Elder Law in New Jersey

ELDER LAW IN NEW JERSEY

FINDING SOLUTIONS FOR LEGAL PROBLEMS

Alice K. Dueker, Esq.

R Rutgers University Press

New Brunswick, New Jersey, and London

Library of Congress Cataloging-in-Publication Data
Dueker, Alice K., 1957–
    Elder law in New Jersey : finding solutions for legal problems /
Alice K. Dueker.
        p.   cm.
    Includes bibliographical references and index.
    ISBN 0-8135-2735-X (cloth : alk. paper). — ISBN 0-8135-2736-8
(paper : alk. paper)
    1. Aged—Legal status, laws, etc.—New Jersey.   I. Title.
KFN1891.A3D84   2000
346.74901′3—dc21   99-32375
                                                              CIP

British Cataloging-in-Publication data for this book is available from
the British Library

Manufactured in the United States of America

To Shelley A. Hearne,
who has never stopped saying "Yes, you can."

Contents

Acknowledgments

I want to thank my colleagues for all their support, which made writing this book possible. I especially want to thank Laurie A. Barron, Jay M. Feinman, Stephen J. Labensky, Anne M. Mullan, and Robert F. Williams. Gail Molina provided invaluable help completing the manuscript. I also owe many thanks to Tom Wuersig, who has contributed immensely to my knowledge of elder law and who has always been both a friend and a resource. I appreciate the generous research support provided to me by Rutgers Law School–Camden, without which I would not have been able to undertake this project. For their able research help I thank Derek Cordier, Adam Hancock, Catherine Miller, Stacey Sammons, Nicole Sovibile, and Mara Speigeland.

Elder Law in New Jersey

Introduction

Old age is not for sissies.
—New Jersey Congresswoman Millicent Fenwick

The population as a whole is aging, and in New Jersey one in five residents is over sixty years old. What does this mean for you? Mostly, this statistic tells us that if you are over sixty, you are not alone. But more than that, it means that there are many others who are experiencing the same range of problems with housing, planning for the future, and dealing with the prospect of increasing disability that comes with age. There are many services available for seniors, but it can often be difficult or confusing to learn what is best for you. You become eligible for government benefits that you could not get when you were younger, and you may need assistance with tasks you are accustomed to doing for yourself. If you are trying to help an older family member or friend, you may find that you have a lot to learn about what is available for seniors. Whether for yourself or for someone else, this book will help you to learn what you can do and where you can get assistance.

This book is intended to help you take advantage of the services that are available to you and to make you aware of when you need to find a lawyer, what kind of help you can expect, and what you can do for yourself without the services of a lawyer. Because the experience of aging often raises these problems, a legal specialty aimed at assisting you has developed, known as elder law. The goal of this specialty is to provide expert legal advice and advocacy geared toward the specific needs of seniors.

I am a teacher and also a lawyer. My goal is to help you understand enough about the law to identify a problem, ask questions that yield useful answers, and either work out the resolution yourself or understand what a lawyer who is helping you is doing and why. Using this book will help you to plan for your future as you get older or help you to assist a friend or family member who is encountering problems resulting from age. There are many resources available to help older New Jerseyans, but it can be difficult to get complete information unless you are very lucky or very persistent. This book is intended to provide some shortcuts and help you to answer some questions yourself or learn where to get more information to use when you need help from someone else.

It can be difficult and frustrating to try to help yourself or a family member or friend with a legal problem. And the legal problems most often encountered by seniors can involve frustrating losses. Sometimes such problems involve the potential loss of control of your own resources or the ability to determine what will happen in your life if your spouse passes away or if other support systems become less able to help and additional assistance is required.

The following chapters address a wide range of issues. The first section, "Benefits," reviews the major benefits programs, including those that pay for medical care, Medicare and Medicaid. An important aspect of obtaining benefits is understanding the process of appealing an unfavorable decision, and this subject is discussed in this section. The second section, "Health Care," looks at various aspects of obtaining and paying for the health care you want. Section III, "Personal Decision Making," discusses writing wills and creating documents to manage your personal affairs if you cannot take care of them yourself. The next section, "Family Concerns," addresses internal family disputes and problems, including grandparent visitation and custody, marriage, divorce, and elder abuse. Section V looks at employment issues: discrimination based on age and disability as well as pensions. Section VI discusses your rights as a consumer and highlights problems of consumer fraud. Since seniors are often targets of fraud, a fact recognized by the creation of an elder fraud task force in New Jersey, it is important that you be aware of your rights and have information available to help you avoid being defrauded. Finally, section VII looks at housing issues for home owners and for tenants. Consideration is given to maintaining and paying for housing, your right to keep pets in rental housing, and using the equity in your home to obtain cash. In addition, this section provides information and resources to help you locate appropriate housing if you need or want a greater range of services and assistance.

Each of these sections includes a number of stories to illustrate the issues discussed. The stories you will find in the following chapters are all based on actual problems faced by real people. The names have been changed to protect the privacy of those involved, and details may have been combined from several similar cases. These stories are included to explain the types of problems that make the legal information given in the book both relevant and necessary. However, no book can cover all the problems encountered by individuals. The discussion of the law in a particular chapter will cover a broad range of problems, of which the story is only one example.

As you read this book you will see that I try to provide you with detailed information about what the law says and how to understand it. Is this enough to allow you to represent yourself or to write your own legal documents? In some circumstances this information should help you to avoid a problem or to understand and solve a problem on your own. But many times the information in this book is not going to address your problem exactly. Or it may address your problem, but not all aspects of your particular situation. In such cases—or if you are having trouble accomplishing what you want to accomplish even if you understand the law—it makes sense to find a lawyer to help you.

DO YOU NEED A LAWYER?

If you think about what lawyers are trained to do, you will understand when a lawyer can be most helpful to you. Lawyers are problem solvers, and they should work with you to determine the extent of any problem and what solutions work for you. No two problems are exactly the same, so the answers lawyers give have to depend on your particular circumstances. Part of the problem with relying on a book like this is that it is impossible to be detailed enough to address all the various alternatives that might apply to you. But a lawyer can describe all your choices and answer your questions.

In addition to trying to help you understand the choices available to you, lawyers are trained to anticipate problems and to think about overlapping issues. For example, some of the actions you might learn about in the following chapters will have tax consequences. I can point out that you should consider whether your taxes will be affected, but I cannot evaluate how much of an effect there will be. An attorney should be able to help you determine what other issues might come up in solving your problem, including any impact on your taxes.

A lawyer is also an advocate for you. When you are having trouble getting someone to pay attention to your problem or you need to persuade others to change their view of your situation, it can help to have someone speak on your behalf. Lawyers are good at this. They can take your position and try to get the other side to see things your way.

If you have trouble speaking up for yourself or you are intimidated by a lawyer on the other side, it can be especially helpful to have someone speak for you. Since it is often easier to argue for someone else than for yourself, you might want someone to help you even if you cannot hire a lawyer. Consider whether it would be enough to have a persuasive friend help you speak up for yourself.

If your problem involves interpreting the law, you are most likely going to want to ask a lawyer to help you make the best possible argument. Lawyers are trained to look at the law, any regulations involved, and the possible interpretations of the law. By reading cases in which courts have decided how to apply the law in the past, a lawyer can help you to fashion an argument that might not be obvious from a statute or regulation itself. Making distinctions between cases can require consideration of subtle variations that would not seem important to most readers. No two cases are exactly alike, and the differences can lead to different outcomes.

Your problem might seem to be covered by one law, but there may be another law that will be relevant. For example, most cases concerning rented property are governed by the state landlord-tenant law, called the New Jersey Anti-Eviction Act. But there are times when federal law is involved. If your case involves discrimination, the federal Fair Housing Act may apply, and without a lawyer you might miss this aspect of the case.

Just about everyone knows what Medicare is, but how many know how to appeal a decision when Medicare says that it will not pay for something? Recently my mother received a letter from Medicare denying a small claim she had submitted. It was not clear to her whether she could challenge the decision or, if so, how to do so. But the process is easy if you know what to do, and I explained that all she had to do was write Medicare, state that she wanted the decision reconsidered, and tell why. If she had not been able to ask me what to do, she would probably have just given up and paid the bill herself. If it had been for a large amount of money, she might have felt that she had to hire an attorney to challenge the decision.

As my mother's situation illustrates, if you take the time to appeal decisions of Medicare or other benefits programs when you believe you are entitled to coverage, you have a very good chance of getting some or all of the charge covered. It is often true that just being willing to speak up, to request a review, or to complain about unfair treatment will be enough to get the result you want. Most people are too intimidated or unwilling to make the effort, and they lose out. But this book will help you to understand what you are entitled to, and it will help you to obtain it. Being willing to speak up for yourself or being persistent enough to get help can go a long way toward solving some of your own problems. Another goal of this book is heading off problems before they become legal issues—or avoiding those problems in the first place.

HOW TO USE THIS BOOK

If you are already facing difficulty with a benefits program or have questions about what you should include in your will, you will find specific sections of this book focused on topics that should answer your questions or at least help you find assistance. But this book is designed to be more useful before such problems arise. It is intended to help you to understand the law on issues likely to concern you at some point in the future and to help you protect yourself from avoidable problems and obtain the benefits to which you are entitled. I recommend that you review each section and look for information that is relevant to you. Start with the questions at the beginning of each section, and read the stories, which give you typical problems and some solutions. If a subject concerns you or addresses something you do not understand, the later section headed "Understanding the Law" will provide more detailed information on the subject. Sources of help are also included if there are resources focused on a particular topic. The appendixes provide more general assistance; in addition to a glossary, they include the addresses and phone numbers of agencies and local offices that are available to help you apply for benefits, interpret information, and get the help you need.

This book is for you if you are dealing with the challenges of aging. Whether you are wondering if there is anything you can do about something that is bothering you or trying to solve a specific legal problem, you will find information in this book that will help you understand your rights. This book may not have all the information you need, but it attempts to help you understand the basics and steer you to more information or sources of assistance. If you are interested in knowing more about how you are affected by the law and how you can protect yourself from being harmed, read on.

I. BENEFITS

Before the Social Security Act was passed in 1935, many people lived their entire lives without any significant interaction with the government and without the need for a lawyer to represent them. But with the introduction of government programs to provide pension benefits and medical care to retirees, this began to change. Now nearly every older American is entitled to some type of benefit. The complexity of the laws and regulations and the problems inherent in providing for so many individuals have spurred the growth of the legal specialty known as elder law.

If you understand how the system of benefits works and for what you are eligible, you will find it much easier to make sense of the information you receive. Government benefits programs strive to provide comprehensive information, but it can nevertheless be difficult to discover how your particular circumstances will be treated. When something goes wrong—for example, you receive money to which you were not actually entitled—understanding your rights to challenge a decision can be crucial.

The chapters in this section cover government benefits and public entitlements: Social Security, Medicare and Medicaid, and other health and medical programs. These chapters address questions such as the following:

- What is the difference between Medicare and Medicaid?
- If I can start receiving Social Security benefits at age sixty-two, why should I continue working until I am sixty-five?
- Social Security sent me a letter saying I received too much money last year. But it was their mistake, and I spent the money. Can I prevent them from taking it back now?
- My spouse has Alzheimer's disease, but does not need to be in a nursing home. Can I get any help with providing care at home?
- My spouse is in the hospital, and we were told Medicare would stop paying the bills in a few days. If more care is necessary, can we challenge this decision?
- Can I get help with my medical bills?

1. Social Security

Social Security is at the heart of the government benefits plan intended to assure each of us a minimum standard of living in retirement. If you have worked, you have paid taxes to support the system, and when you retire you are entitled to receive benefits. This chapter addresses questions about who can receive benefits and about what benefits are available.

Social Security provides retirement benefits to workers and also to the spouses of workers. It provides survivors' benefits, and it provides benefits to disabled workers and their dependents. In addition, through the Supplemental Security Income (SSI) program a welfare benefit is provided to low-income people who are elderly or disabled. It is important to understand what benefits you are entitled to receive so that you can be certain you receive the maximum benefits for which you are eligible. There are also times when it is necessary to appeal a Social Security decision, and you should understand the process for doing this.

RETIREMENT BENEFITS

You are entitled to Social Security benefits if you have worked and paid Social Security taxes for ten years. Each year you work, you receive credits toward your benefits by earning a certain amount of money, and that amount is adjusted annually. In 1999, for example, you earned one credit for each $740 you earned, up to a maximum of four credits a year. Once you had forty credits, you would be entitled to receive benefits.

The amount of the benefits you may receive is decided by a complicated formula based on your average monthly income. You will be eligible to begin receiving a reduced benefit at age sixty-two. If you were born before 1938 and you wait to begin receiving benefits until you are sixty-five, you will receive your full benefit. Those born after 1938 will have to wait longer in order to receive the full benefit; the retirement age is slowly being increased. When the age increase is fully implemented (for those born in 1960), the age for full benefits will be sixty-seven.

If you continue working and do not collect Social Security benefits when you turn sixty-five, you will receive a small percentage increase in your benefit for each month that you work past the full retirement age. But if you work past age sixty-five and also receive benefits, your benefit will be decreased by a percentage of the amount you earn. If you work and receive Social Security benefits, if you are under sixty-five, you can earn $9,120 before your benefits will be affected; over that amount, you will lose $1 in benefits for each $2 you earn. If you are between sixty-five and sixty-nine, you can earn $14,500; if you earn more, you will lose $1 in benefits for each $3 you earn. Once you are seventy, there will be no reduction in your benefits if you work. Make sure you understand how much you can earn and what you will lose if you keep working while you receive benefits.

To apply for your retirement benefits, contact your local Social Security office. You can apply over the telephone, but you will have to provide documentation to establish your eligibility. You should apply three months before your birthday if you want to receive benefits before you turn sixty-five. That will give Social Security time to process your application. No retroactive benefits are paid if you are applying for early retirement benefits.

If your spouse worked, you are entitled to spousal benefits. The amount you receive will be a percentage of what your spouse receives. If you worked in low-paying jobs or did not work for many years, the spousal benefit may be higher than what you are entitled to based on your own earning record. If you think this may be the case, ask Social Security which benefit will be higher, one based on your earning record or a spousal benefit based on your spouse's earning record. You can receive whichever benefit is higher, but not both.

If you are divorced, you may still be entitled to receive benefits based on your former spouse's earnings, even if your spouse is not receiving benefits. As long as both of you are old enough for benefits, you can receive them. If you remarry you cannot base your benefits claim on your prior spouse's earnings record. You may also be entitled to survivors' benefits, even though you are divorced.

SURVIVORS' BENEFITS

If you are entitled to benefits at the time of your death, your family members are entitled to survivors' benefits whether or not you have begun receiving payments. The amount they receive will vary, depending on their ages and their relationships to you. For example, if at the time of your death your spouse is sixty-five or older, he or she will receive 100 percent of your benefits. But if your spouse is between sixty and sixty-four, he or she will be eligible for between 71 and 94 percent of your benefits. If you have minor children, they will be entitled to benefits.

If the amount your spouse is entitled to as a survivor is higher than his or her own benefit, he or she should choose to receive that benefit. If the amount of your spouse's own benefit is higher, there is no reason for him or her to receive the survivor benefit. Your spouse cannot receive both retirement and survivors' benefits. It is also possible to change benefits; for example, your spouse can receive survivors' benefits before he or she is sixty-five and then switch to retirement benefits at the full rate at age sixty-five. A Social Security representative should be able to help your spouse determine his or her eligibility.

OVERPAYMENTS

If you receive Social Security benefits to which you are not entitled, the Social Security Administration must ask you to repay the excess benefits. You will receive a notice, and you will have three avenues available to you:

- Pay the amount determined to be an overpayment.
- Appeal the decision that there has been an overpayment. Repayment will be delayed until the appeal is decided. If you think the basis for the decision is incorrect, this route makes sense.
- Request a waiver of repayment. If the reason for the overpayment was not your fault and it would be a financial hardship for you to repay the money you received, you may not have to pay it back. For a waiver to be granted, you must not have done anything to cause the overpayment and you must not have been aware that there was an overpayment. If you gave Social Security accurate information but your benefit was figured incorrectly, you may be entitled to a waiver. But if you received an extra payment and you should have known that you were not entitled to it, you will have to repay the amount.

The notice you receive from Social Security will tell you about your right to appeal or request a waiver. If you appeal, write an explanation as to why you think the decision is wrong and attach any documents that will support your position. Social Security officials will reconsider their decision. If they still think you received too much in benefits, you are entitled to request a hearing. If instead of appealing the decision you request a waiver, be prepared to show why it would be a hardship to pay the money back. You can first appeal the decision and then, if you lose the appeal, request a waiver. Just be sure that you did not do anything to cause the overpayment.

SOCIAL SECURITY DISABILITY INSURANCE (SSDI) BENEFITS

Jesus has worked in construction for thirty-five years, and he is now sixty-one years old. He recently had surgery on both his knees because arthritis was causing him increasing pain and difficulty walking. He now walks with a cane and is pleased to be able to get around, but he cannot bend or move quickly. He knows that he cannot return to construction work, and he does not think that he can do any other work. He has called the Social Security office and been told that if he waits until he is sixty-two he will receive 80 percent of the benefits he would have received at sixty-five.

Jesus may be entitled to receive Social Security disability insurance benefits. In addition to having worked the required number of months for an employer who paid Social Security taxes, he must be able to establish that he is unable to do any paid work. This process will require that he establish that his medical condition is severe enough to prevent him from doing any job at all, but it will also take into consideration his age, education, and work experience. The process of establishing eligibility can be difficult and time consuming, but if Jesus succeeds in receiving benefits he will receive them as of the date he became unable to work. If the Social Security Administration initially denies his claim and he ultimately wins, he will receive a retroactive benefit award.

Jesus will realize two additional advantages to receiving disability benefits rather than waiting until he is eligible for retirement benefits. First, he will receive a full benefit based on his entire earning record rather than the reduced benefit he would have received for retiring early at age sixty-two. The disability benefit will treat him as if he had retired at sixty-five. Second, he will become eligible for Medicare after two years rather than having to wait until he is sixty-five.

The process for determining if you are entitled to disability benefits is complex, and it can be extremely slow. You must establish that you cannot work because you have a severe disabling condition. The Social Security Administration will consider whether you can return to your former job and also whether there are any other jobs you could do. If you are initially denied benefits, you are well advised to appeal; a significant number of initial denials are later reversed. You might want to seek legal advice if you are denied disability benefits you think you should receive.

GETTING HELP

You may be entitled to free representation if you must appeal to receive disability benefits. Contact your county Office on Aging or Legal Services office to find out if you can obtain free representation. If not, a lawyer may be willing to represent you in a disability appeal without any initial payment from you. If you win benefits, the lawyer will take as payment a percentage of any retroactive benefits you receive. To find a lawyer with expertise in this area, call the National Organization of Social Security Claimants' Representatives at (800) 431-2804 or write them at 6 Prospect Street, Midland Park, NJ 07432. Before the representation begins, make sure you understand any fee agreement you sign.

2. Medicare and Medicaid

What are Medicare and Medicaid? How are they different? Will they pay for the medical care I need? Will they take care of me if I have to enter a nursing home? Although almost everyone knows something about these programs, many of us still have questions like these. It is inevitable that as we age we will require more medical care, and it is impossible to ignore the reality of the costs of receiving this care. Since the provision of medical insurance in the United States is largely tied to employment, once you retire from work or stop working because of disability you "fall out" of the regular system of paying for care.

In an innovative move, in 1965 Congress put into place the first national health insurance program, Medicare. Today seniors rely on Medicare coverage to pay for a substantial percentage of their medical needs. But Medicare alone will not cover all the costs of receiving care. It is important to understand what is and is not covered by Medicare and also what alternatives or additions to Medicare will assist you with paying for treatment. Medicaid, a state and federal program that is generally seen as a resource to use to pay for long-term care, is equally complex and hard to understand. But a basic understanding of both these programs will help you to be sure you are receiving the benefits to which you are entitled and to negotiate the U.S. health care system with a minimum of hassle.

DIFFERENCES BETWEEN MEDICARE AND MEDICAID

Claudia, age seventy-two, was brought to the hospital after collapsing at home, and she was disoriented. She had not broken anything, but she had some bruises. She was found to be severely dehydrated, and it was determined that she overdosed on her medication. It has taken eight days of treatment in the hospital to stabilize Claudia, and the doctor has stated that she will require skilled nursing care upon release. The doctor has said that Claudia will not be able to return home right away or to live on her own again because she is unable to care for herself properly. The doctor has advised Claudia's son to look into a nursing home. But if Claudia has to pay for a nursing home, her assets will soon be depleted.

Claudia's nursing home care will be paid for by Medicare if her case meets these strict requirements: she must have been a hospital inpatient for at least three days prior to admission to the nursing home, she must be admitted to the nursing home within thirty days of the date she was discharged from the hospital, and she must require skilled nursing care. Skilled nursing care is care that must be provided in a skilled nursing facility to a patient who requires professional inpatient treatment. It includes physical and speech therapy. If Claudia does not require this type of care and instead needs assistance with activities of daily living such as bathing and dressing, Medicare will not provide payment for nursing home care. Medicaid will provide coverage if Claudia is otherwise eligible.

COVERAGE. The basic difference between Medicare and Medicaid is that Medicare is insurance intended to cover accidents and illnesses. Medicare coverage is not provided for long-term, chronic conditions. Medicaid, on the other hand, is a welfare program that covers all kinds of care, including long-term care, for those who cannot afford to pay for care themselves. Since the costs of long-term care are very high, a chronic condition that requires a high level of care, such as the care provided by a nursing home, often exhausts the resources of patients who can pay initially.

It is important to realize that someone who can get by financially with Medicare covering the costs of acute illness may become eligible for Medicaid after a period of time. In the example above, Claudia will be covered by Medicare initially for her nursing home care. But after a period of time her condition will deteriorate. She will no longer need skilled nursing care, but she will need constant care. If she does not require skilled nursing care, Medicare will stop paying. Once she has spent all of her own money paying for nursing home care, she will become eligible for Medicaid.

ELIGIBILITY. You are eligible for Medicare if you are over sixty-five and you or your spouse has worked for ten years in a job or jobs that have paid Social Security taxes or you are entitled to Railroad Retirement benefits, the equivalent of Social Security for those who were railroad employees. This is the same standard that determines eligibility for Social Security benefits, so if Congress changes the age of eligibility for Social Security benefits it is likely to also change the standard for Medicare. You are also eligible for Medicare if you have been disabled under the Social Security definition for two years or you require dialysis for kidney failure. If you have not worked long enough but you are a United States citizen or a permanent alien and have lived in the United States for at least five years, you are entitled to purchase Medicare coverage by paying a premium.

Eligibility for Medicaid is more complex. Medicaid is a state and federal program that pays medical bills for needy people who are eligible. To qualify for Medicaid you must be sixty-five or older or must be blind or disabled. To qualify as blind or disabled you must be eligible for Supplemental Security Income (SSI) benefits. If you receive SSI benefits, you are automatically eligible for Medicaid. If you do not qualify for SSI, you may still receive Medicaid if your income is below the federal poverty level and your assets are below a certain level. (In 1999, a single person could not have an income above $8,292 per year, and a couple could not have an income above $11,100 per year. This number is adjusted annually.)

In addition to meeting the income limits, you cannot own property worth more than $4,000 for one person or $6,000 for a couple. Again, the resource limit is adjusted periodically. This includes money in bank accounts and investments. It does not include the home you live in, your household goods or personal property, a car, or a life insurance policy with a face value of less than $1,500 per person.

Medicaid will pay for nursing home care if you are or become "medically needy." This means that you have too much income and too many resources to qualify for SSI, but your medical expenses qualify you for assistance. This is often the case if you require long-term care in a nursing home and do not have sufficient insurance or resources to pay for the care yourself.

MEDICARE

There are two parts to traditional Medicare. Part A helps pay for hospital treatment, care in a nursing home, home health care, and hospice care (see box, top of next page). Part B helps pay for doctors, outpatient hospital care, and some other medical services not covered by Part A. Everyone who receives Medicare gets Part A. You must choose Part B (or an alternative, Medicare+Choice, discussed later), and you must pay a premium.

WHAT IS COVERED BY
MEDICARE PART A?

Medicare Part A covers a wide range of treatments:

- Inpatient hospital care, including
    A semiprivate room
    Meals
    Nursing services
    Drugs
    Lab tests and supplies
    X-rays
- Psychiatric hospitalization
- Care at a Christian Science sanatorium
- Care at a skilled nursing facility (nursing home)
- Home health care, including
    Aide services
    Durable medical equipment
- Hospice care

EXCLUSIONS FROM MEDICARE COVERAGE. Medicare will not pay for cosmetic surgery, most dental care, routine checkups, "custodial" care (most nursing home care), or services that are "not medically reasonable or necessary for the diagnosis or treatment of illness or injury" (42 U.S.C.A. 1395[a][1][A]). A decision by Medicare that something is to be excluded, usually because it is found to be "not reasonable and necessary," can be appealed, and often you will be successful. See the section on appeals.

PREMIUMS, DEDUCTIBLES, AND CO-PAYMENTS. The monthly premium for Part B is currently $45.50, which is deducted from your Social Security, Railroad Retirement, or Civil Service Retirement check. Part B provides coverage for a wide range of medical services and supplies, including doctor visits, outpatient hospital services, x-rays and lab tests, ambulance transportation, physical therapy, flu shots, outpatient mental health treatment, wheelchairs, walkers, and medical supplies such as ostomy bags, surgical dressings, and casts. There are specific requirements for and

---

HOSPICE CARE

If you are terminally ill you have the option to choose hospice care instead of regular Medicare. The emphasis of hospice services is on providing comfort and relief from pain. Services are usually provided in your home and include homemaker services, counseling service, and the provision of certain prescription drugs, in addition to doctor and nursing services. For further information, see chapter 4.

---

limitations on Medicare coverage. For example, ambulance transportation is covered only when transportation in any other vehicle could endanger your health. Both Part A and Part B benefits are limited by a number of exclusions, deductibles, and co-payment requirements, discussed in the next section. Overall, Medicare pays roughly half of all medical bills for those who are receiving both parts.

Medicare requires you to share the costs of your medical coverage. If you choose Part B coverage, you pay to participate in the program by paying a monthly premium. Deductibles require you to pay up to a certain dollar amount before Medicare begins to cover the services you receive. You pay the first $100 per year for Part B services, and you pay the first $768 (adjusted annually) for each period of hospitalization before Part A coverage begins.

Finally, Medicare does not cover the full cost of services you receive, so you must make "co-payments" for the balance of the cost. Medicare usually covers 80 percent of Part B costs. For hospitalization you pay $192 per day after sixty days, and a larger amount after ninety days. In order to cover these expenses, you should either purchase Medigap insurance or find out if you are eligible for a government program that will cover some or all of the costs. See the section headed "Assistance with the Costs of Medicare."

ENROLLMENT. You are automatically enrolled in Medicare if you are receiving Social Security or Railroad Retirement benefits at the time you turn sixty-five. If you are not receiving benefits, you need to apply for Medicare. Even if you continue working and do not receive Social

> ## WHERE TO CALL FOR
> ## MORE INFORMATION
>
> ■ For information on Medicare coverage and choosing Medigap insurance, contact Counseling on Health Insurance for Medicare Enrollees (CHIME) at (800) 792-8820.
> ■ For information on Medicare coverage and Part B claims, contact Medicare Carrier—Xact Medicare Services at (800) 462-9306.
> ■ For information on Medicare coverage of durable medical equipment (such as wheelchairs and hospital beds), contact United Health Care Insurance Company at (800) 842-2052.

Security at age sixty-five, you may want to apply for Medicare. You should apply three months before your birthday to avoid a possible delay in the start of Part B coverage. If you do not apply by your sixty-fifth birthday, the premiums increase. If you are covered by an employer plan, Medicare can be a secondary insurer until your seventieth birthday, when it becomes the primary insurer.

SUPPLEMENTAL INSURANCE YOU MAY NEED. Since Medicare pays for only part of all medical care, it is still important to purchase medical insurance to make up the difference. There are two kinds of insurance that you should consider. The first and more usual kind is generally referred to as Medigap insurance. The second is long-term care insurance, which is discussed in chapter 5. Medigap insurance is private insurance that is designed to help pay Medicare co-payment amounts. There are ten standard policies, and each offers a different combination of benefits. The best time to buy a policy is during the open enrollment period. For six months from the date you are first enrolled in Medicare Part B and you are sixty-five or older, you have the right to buy the Medigap policy of your choice. You cannot be turned down because of poor health if you buy a policy during this period. Once the open Medigap enrollment ends, you may have to accept whatever Medigap policy an insurance company is willing to sell you.

THE NEW MEDICARE + CHOICE PROGRAM. New options for receiving Medicare services are being developed under the Medicare+Choice program. This program, which began in 1999, allows you to choose one of several different ways to receive services. These include Medicare health maintenance organizations (HMOs), preferred provider organizations (PPOs), and medical savings accounts. At this point most of the choices available in New Jersey are HMOs. These organizations may charge no more than the Part B premium or may have monthly fees. They cover doctor visits with a $5 to $15 co-payment. They usually offer additional benefits, such as coverage for some prescription drugs or dental exams. You are generally required to choose a participating doctor and hospital, and your access to specialists may be limited.

Medicare+Choice is intended to encourage the development of multiple options so that you can find the one that best meets your needs. One new option is the use of medical savings accounts, which have been introduced on a limited basis. These combine insurance with high deductible amounts ($6,000 in 1999) with savings accounts to cover routine care. The goal is cost savings along with more choice and flexibility than an HMO.

There are several things to keep in mind about Medicare+Choice. First, traditional Medicare is still available, and you do not have to choose an HMO or any other option. Second, if you choose an HMO be sure you understand what will be included and what limitations you will face. If you travel a lot or spend part of the year in another state, make sure you will receive coverage when you need it. The typical HMO, for example, covers only emergency care when you are out of the HMO's geographic area.

A lot is unknown about how the Medicare+Choice options will work. They represent a major change in the Medicare program, and only time will show their effectiveness. If you make a change, consider what will happen if you are not satisfied. If you give up Medigap insurance for an HMO, for example, you might have to pay a higher price if you do not like the HMO and want to return to your original option.

Because of the high cost of Medicare, it is likely that new choices will continue to be offered as efforts are made to give people the health care coverage they need at a price that is affordable. It is very important that you understand what will be included before you decide which choice is right for you. Pay attention to what will happen if your medical needs are greater in the future; an option that makes sense when you

---

**WHERE TO FIND MORE INFORMATION
ABOUT MEDICARE+CHOICE**

Information on Medicare+Choice is available by phone at (800)
318-2596 or on the Internet at www.medicare.gov.

---

are generally healthy may not be as valuable if you are seriously ill. Also
consider what will happen as you get older. Some options guarantee
not to raise your premiums as you age, but others do not. If you are
having trouble figuring out what is right for you, contact the services
listed in the boxes on this page and page 19 or under "Getting Help."
Counseling about insurance options is available, and it is free.

ASSISTANCE WITH THE COSTS OF MEDICARE. If you receive Medicare
and have a very low income and few assets, you may qualify for
assistance with paying your health care costs through two programs.
One is called the Qualified Medicare Beneficiary (QMB) program,
whereas the other is called the Specified Low-Income Medicare Beneficiary (SLMB) program. These programs are not as restricted as
Medicaid, but they also cover less.

If you get Medicare Part A and your income is at or below the
national poverty level, the QMB program pays Medicare's premiums,
deductibles, and co-insurance. In order to qualify, your savings and
other assets cannot exceed $4,000 for one person or $6,000 for a couple.
The monthly income limits for the QMB program at the time of this
writing are $691 for an individual and $925 for a couple.

The SLMB program is for people entitled to Medicare Part A
whose income is 20 percent higher than the national poverty level. The
program pays only your Medicare Part B premium; you still have to pay
deductibles. The monthly income limits at present are $825 for an
individual and $1,105 for a couple.

If you have Medicare Part A and you think you qualify for one of
these programs, you must file an application for Medicaid.

GETTING HELP. Counseling on Health Insurance for Medicare Enrollees (CHIME) provides free information and counseling. Call (800)
792-8820.

APPEALING MEDICARE DENIALS

Jorge has throat cancer. Following radiation treatments his teeth deteriorated, and several of his teeth have had to be removed. When the dental work was done, Jorge submitted the bill to Medicare just as he had submitted other bills for his cancer treatment. When Medicare denied payment for the dental work, his dentist contacted Medicare to advocate on his behalf and was told that Medicare does not cover dental work unless it is required by medical treatment. Medicare took the position that if the teeth had been removed prior to the radiation treatment it would have covered the work, but that it was not clear that the removal of the teeth was related to the cancer, and therefore it did not have to pay.

Jorge appealed the Medicare denial. In his favor is the fact that standard medical treatment for his cancer requires that efforts be made to save as many teeth as possible. Therefore, doctors advise that no teeth should be pulled until the radiation treatment is complete and it is possible to observe the health of the teeth. This argument was accepted by the hearing judge, but Medicare refused to accept this determination and overturned the administrative law judge's decision. Unfortunately, the next step in the appeals process, appeal to the federal court, requires that the amount being disputed be more than $1,000. Because the dental work cost $750, Jorge has no further right of appeal.

UNDERSTANDING THE LAW. Jorge's story underscores the difficulties that can come up when appealing Medicare denials. But it should not discourage you from trying. It is important to understand what Medicare is looking for in the appeals process, how the process works, and the need for patience, since it can sometimes be a lengthy process. But, especially if your claim is substantial, it can be worthwhile to stand up for your rights, especially when your doctor supports your position.

You have the right to appeal Medicare denials. You may have to go through several steps, but do not give up. Many appeals are successful. The exact steps in the process and the amount of money that has to be involved vary depending on the type of case. This information is summarized in the paragraphs that follow.

THE IMPORTANCE OF FILING A CLAIM

It is important to file a claim—or have a Medicare provider file a claim for you—even if the provider thinks it will be denied. Unless you have made the request, there will be nothing to appeal. So insist that a claim be filed whenever you want to seek coverage.

It is not difficult to appeal an unfavorable decision, and it often pays off. You will receive information about appealing Medicare's decision. Just write a letter, including a copy of the claim denial, and explain why you think the decision is wrong. If additional information is relevant, include it in your letter. Keep copies of everything you send.

There are time limits for each stage of the appeals process. Usually you have at least sixty days—and sometimes six months—from the date of the denial to request the next step in the appeal. Even if you wait longer you can sometimes argue that there was a good reason and your appeal will be allowed. For example, if you did not receive a notice because it was sent to the wrong address, you might be able to argue "good cause" for filing late. But if you can avoid it, do not wait until the last minute to request your appeal. It will only delay the process. It can take a long time to get a decision once you have made a request.

The typical appeal begins with reconsideration or review of the claim. The initial decision is made by an insurance company that has the Medicare contract to process claims. This step of the appeal process requires the insurance company that made the initial decision to take a second look. You can submit additional written information, so write a letter explaining why you think the initial decision was wrong.

If your claim is denied again and the amount in dispute is more than $100, you are entitled to a fair hearing. This is provided by a hearing officer of the carrier and can be conducted in person or on the telephone. It is not like a court hearing, so it is relatively informal. The goal is to obtain all the evidence that will help the hearing officer make a decision, which can include information from you or from your doctor.

If you still have not received the coverage you think you are entitled to after a fair hearing, you can request an administrative

---

IF YOU ARE A HOSPITAL INPATIENT

When you are admitted to a hospital you should receive a written notice of your rights, including your right to appeal decisions about payment for your care. If you are notified during your hospital stay that services will no longer be covered by Medicare, you are entitled to *immediate* review by a peer review organization (PRO). This is an organization of physicians that will review the decision and determine your need for continuing care in the hospital.

---

hearing. This is a more formal hearing, on the record and with sworn testimony. Depending on what part of Medicare is involved, your claim will have to be for over $100 or for as much as $500 to have a hearing. You might want an attorney to assist you at this stage, but without one you can still present the issues you think the judge should consider and any additional evidence you think is relevant. You can also object to evidence that should not be in the record if, for example, it is inaccurate for some objective reason. You cannot object to evidence just because you do not agree with it.

A lawyer can be helpful in an administrative hearing, because the outcome of the hearing may rest on how the judge interprets the Medicare law and regulations. In Jorge's case, described earlier, Medicare said that his dental work should not be covered because the work was not medically necessary. His lawyers argued that up-to-date medical information showed that the steps taken by his doctors were appropriate and that the practice recommended by Medicare, removing his teeth before radiation, was now disfavored. This argument persuaded the administrative law judge to find in Jorge's favor.

Once the administrative law judge has made a decision, it is reviewed by the Appeals Council. It was at this stage that Jorge lost, because the board disagreed with the judge's decision. If the Appeals Council denies your claim, the next step is to appeal to the federal court. At this point your claim must be worth at least $1,000 and in some cases $2,000. If your claim, like Jorge's, is for less, there is nothing more that you can do.

MEDICAID

As a supplement to Medicare, Medicaid pays for certain services not covered by Medicare and also provides necessary medical care when Medicare benefits are exhausted. Your Medicare benefits must be used up before Medicaid will pay for your health care services.

ESTABLISHING ELIGIBILITY. Establishing financial eligibility for Medicaid involves a detailed process of reviewing your income and assets. The Medicaid administrator will look at not only what you own at the time you apply, but also your financial transactions for the previous three years. If you have other health insurance, you must report that when applying for Medicaid benefits so that Medicaid can make sure that all sources of payment for medical services are used before Medicaid pays a bill. The specifics of this review process are discussed in chapter 5.

HOW MEDICAID WORKS. Once you are found eligible for Medicaid, you will receive an identification card. You may go to any participating provider to receive services. You will then be asked to sign a form listing the service that was provided. (Do not sign any blank form!) The provider will send the bill to Medicaid for payment. Medicaid may ask you to complete a form and return it, describing what service was given. This to ensure that what appears on the bill was actually the service you received.

You must notify the county welfare agency whenever there is a change in your income, you receive additional income, or you gain access to a new resource such as income from a new job or a change in wages, Social Security or Veterans' Benefits, pension or other retirement benefits, accident claims or settlements, an inheritance of money or property, or lottery winnings or other awards.

When you receive Medicaid you must agree to assign to the state any rights to payment from any third party, such as those listed in the preceding paragraph. You also must authorize the county welfare agency to contact any source that may have knowledge of your finances—including the Internal Revenue Service (IRS) and Social Security (for information from your wage and benefits files). Medicaid may contact these sources for the sole purpose of verifying the statements made on your application.

SERVICES COVERED BY MEDICAID

In New Jersey Medicaid covers many services and products, including:

- Physician services
- Services from chiropractors, dentists, certified midwives, podiatrists, psychologists, and optometrists
- Prescribed drugs from a pharmacy
- Hospital inpatient and outpatient care
- Home health care, nursing home care, and medical day care as planned by the patient's doctor
- HMO services available in certain areas
- Physical, speech-language, or occupational therapy as prescribed by a doctor
- Mental health services
- Eyeglasses, hearing aids, artificial limbs, and braces
- Medical supplies and equipment
- X-ray and laboratory services
- Ambulance and coach services for persons with disabilities as prescribed by a doctor
- Transportation to and from Medicaid-approved health care services when it is not otherwise available
- Personal care assistant services

APPEALING A MEDICAID DECISION. If you are denied Medicaid benefits, told your eligibility is coming to an end, or told that a medical procedure or device will not be covered by Medicaid, you can request a hearing to review that decision. In order to appeal you must contact the agency in your county responsible for Medicaid. Do this right away. You have twenty days to request a hearing, but if you make the request within ten days, in some circumstances you will be entitled to continue your benefits while you appeal. Make sure you make your request in writing, and ask specifically for your benefits to be continued while your appeal is being decided.

Requesting a hearing means that you will have a chance to argue to an administrative law judge that you should get the benefits you seek.

Like a hearing for a Medicare appeal, this will be a hearing where a judge will hear testimony and take evidence, including documents and medical records, but it will not be as formal as a trial. No one representing Medicaid will be at the hearing. It should be the intent of you and your attorney, if you have one, to show the judge that your argument is a correct interpretation of the law governing Medicaid. Although the hearing will not be formal, it will be important for you or anyone representing you to understand the Medicaid law and regulations. The judge should decide within ninety days whether your interpretation of the Medicaid law is correct. If your appeal is denied at this level, you can continue to appeal, next to the Division of Medical Assistance and Health Services and, if necessary, to the Appellate Division of the New Jersey Superior Court.

3. Health and Medical Programs in New Jersey

This chapter describes a number of programs available to assist elderly New Jersey residents. Programs are available to assist you in paying the high costs of premiums, co-payments, and prescription drugs. Other programs are intended to keep you in your home and out of a nursing home as long as possible.

THE MEDICALLY NEEDY PROGRAM

This program assists certain New Jersey residents who are not eligible for Medicaid to receive medical care and services. It is designed for those with excessive medical bills that cause their income to be "spent down" to $367 per month for a one-person household and $434 per month for a two-person household. This program offers basically the same services as Medicaid.

If you are spending a great deal of your income on medical bills, this program may be for you. It is administered through the Division of Medical Assistance and Health Services of the New Jersey Department of Human Services. Contact your county Board of Social Services or county welfare agency.

THE COMMUNITY CARE PROGRAM FOR THE ELDERLY AND DISABLED (CCPED)

This is a special Medicaid program that offers a variety of community-based services to help eligible individuals remain in or return to the community rather than being cared for in a nursing facility. You may be eligible if you meet the following standards:

- You are sixty-five or older or determined to be eligible for Social Security disability benefits.
- You are not already receiving Medicaid services in your community.
- Your medical needs meet certain criteria established by the New Jersey Medicaid program.
- Your income and assets meet the financial guidelines of the program. Depending on your income, you may be asked to share in the cost of the program.

For information call the Division of Senior Affairs of the New Jersey Department of Health and Senior Services at (609) 588-2906 or contact your county Board of Social Services or county Welfare Board.

THE HOME CARE EXPANSION PROGRAM

This program offers assistance to eligible individuals who are elderly or disabled and who require medically necessary home care to help them avoid institutionalization. The program offers a comprehensive assessment of your need for long-term home care and develops a plan of care. Its services include home health care, medical day care, nonemergency medical transportation, case management, social adult day care, homemaker care, and respite care. The cost of your care will be limited to an annual amount based on a percentage of the average cost of nursing home care. You may be required to share in the cost of services if your monthly income exceeds a standard monthly maintenance allowance.

Eligibility criteria include the following:

- You are sixty-five or older or have been found to be disabled by the Social Security Administration or by the Bureau of Medical Affairs of the New Jersey Department of Human Services.
- You are eligible for Medicare benefits or are covered by other medical insurance that includes physician and hospitalization coverage.
- Your annual gross income is under $18,000 if you are single or under $21,000 if you are married.
- You are not already receiving comparable assistance and obtaining home care services under Medicaid.
- Your resources are less than $15,000 in liquid assets, regardless of whether you are single or married.

For more information write the Division of Medical Assistance and Health Services of the New Jersey Department of Human Services at CN-715, Trenton, NJ 08625-0715, or call (609) 588-7031 or (800) 792-9745.

HEALTH CARE ASSISTANCE PROGRAMS

New Jersey offers several programs to ensure that eligible seniors receive needed medical care and services. There are income and asset limits for most of these programs.

PHARMACEUTICAL ASSISTANCE TO THE AGED AND DISABLED (PAAD).
If you are over age sixty-five or you receive Social Security disability benefits and your income is below $18,150 for a single person or below $22,256 for a married couple, you are entitled to insurance coverage that provides prescription drugs. You must also be a permanent New Jersey resident and have been in the state for thirty days before you apply, and you cannot have better prescription coverage from another source. If you have other coverage that is more limited than the PAAD program, you are still eligible for these benefits.

Once you qualify you will pay only $5 for each prescription you fill. The program covers drugs, insulin, and certain diabetic testing materials, as long as they are medically necessary and prescribed by a doctor. You can receive a thirty-four-day supply or 100 unit doses, whichever costs more, at one time. The drugs must be FDA approved, they must be purchased in New Jersey, and the manufacturer must have agreed to provide the state with rebates.

HEARING AID ASSISTANCE TO THE AGED AND DISABLED (HAAD). If you
are eligible to receive assistance for prescriptions through the PAAD program, you are also entitled to a benefit of $100 to reimburse you for the purchase of a hearing aid.

NEW JERSEY CARE. New Jersey offers full Medicaid coverage to New
Jersey residents who are sixty-five or older and to those who are blind

---

HEALTH CARE ASSISTANCE PROGRAMS

Health care assistance programs are administered by the Division of Senior Affairs of the New Jersey Department of Health and Senior Services. You can write them at CN-360, Trenton, NJ 08625-0360.

APPLYING FOR PAAD AND HAAD BENEFITS

Applications are available at senior citizens' centers, Medicaid offices, and local pharmacies. For more information write the PAAD Program or HAAD Program, Division of Senior Affairs, New Jersey Department of Health and Senior Services, CN-715, Trenton, NJ 08625-0715, or call (800) 792-9745.

or receiving Social Security disability benefits and meet the income and asset guidelines. This means you must have a monthly income of less than $691 for an individual or $925 for a couple and assets of under $4,000 if you are single or $6,000 for a couple (see chapter 2 for details). For information contact your county Board of Social Services or county Welfare Board.

THE PERSONAL ASSISTANCE SERVICES PROGRAM. This program provides assistance to New Jersey residents between the ages of eighteen and sixty-five who have physical disabilities. Participants are provided with up to forty hours per week of personal assistance services to assist them with routine nonmedical tasks that are directly related to maintaining their health and independence in order to be employed or receive training or education related to employment or to support community-based independent living. The services provided include assistance with bathing, dressing, preparation of meals, shopping, and transportation. The program is designed to help you if you have no one available to help care for you. Some participants pay no fee; others pay a portion of the cost on a sliding fee scale.

If you are between the ages of sixty and sixty-five, contact your county Office on Aging for information. Everyone else should write to the county Office for the Disabled or the Office of Adult Services of the Division of Youth and Family Services, New Jersey Department of Human Services, at CN-717, Trenton, NJ 08625-0717, or call (609) 984-7752.

RESPITE CARE. This program provides relief caregiving services to frail elderly people or to people age eighteen and older who are functionally impaired. These services provide relief from the physical and emotional demands of caregiving to family members and other uncompensated people who are serving as caregivers and are experiencing fatigue and stress due to long-term caregiving. The services are intermittent, short term, and temporary. They include the following:

- Companion services.
- Homemaker or home health aide services.
- Medical adult day care.
- Social adult day care.
- Short-term inpatient care in a licensed medical facility.

Receipt of services is decided by a system that gives priority to families in which the member being cared for is at risk of long-term institutionalization because the caregiver is unable to continue in that role. If you are the person receiving care, your income is the only income considered for eligibility, and the monthly income limit is $1,482. Your assets may not exceed $40,000. Co-payments are required if your income or assets are over the eligibility requirements. In the event that you and another individual in your home both require respite care, your joint income will be taken into consideration when determining your eligibility for this program.

The state administers the overall program. However, the county Offices on Aging assess individuals' eligibility and provide the services. Contact your county Office on Aging for more information.

ADULT DAY CARE FOR THOSE WITH ALZHEIMER'S DISEASE. The state provides specialized programs statewide that serve people with chronic progressive diseases causing dementia. Under this type of program the state pays participating day care centers 75 percent of the daily cost, and the person served pays the remaining 25 percent. If you cannot pay, the participating day care center may determine that other resources are available. If you are funded, you may attend up to three days per week. The purpose of such programs is to provide families with support and to assist older adults who are impaired to maintain their level of functioning and enhance their quality of life.

Criteria for eligibility include the following:

- You must have been diagnosed by a licensed physician as having Alzheimer's disease or a related disorder, such as a multi-infarct

dementia, Parkinson's disease with dementia, Huntington's disease, Cruetzfeldt-Jacob's disease, or Pick's disease.
- You must be cared for or supervised by a family member or other informal caregiver.
- You must be residing in the community, but not as a resident of a rooming house or boarding home.
- Your annual gross income must be less than $15,162 if you are single, less than $19,827 for a couple living with others, and less than $24,493 for a couple living alone.

The services that are offered under this type of program include the following:

- Health monitoring.
- Counseling.
- Recreation.
- Socialization.
- Provision of nutritional meals.
- Support group participation.
- Provision of information and referrals.

To determine whether this type of program is offered in your community, contact your county Office on Aging. This type of program is administered through the Division of Senior Affairs of the Department of Health and Senior Services. You may write to the division at CN-364, Trenton, NJ 08625-0364, or call (609) 292-5037.

HOSPITAL RESPITE CARE PROGRAMS FOR SENIOR CITIZENS. A hospital with an average weekend vacancy rate of 20 percent or more over a six-month period may establish a hospital respite care program. Under this type of program otherwise empty hospital facilities may be used to provide food, shelter, recreation, and supervision to people who are dependent mainly on family members or others for their care. Hospitals offering this type of program may opt to offer it weekdays as well as weekends. To find out if this type of program is offered in your area, contact your county Office on Aging.

THE NURSING HOME PREADMISSION SCREENING PROGRAM. This program determines the needs of Medicaid-eligible individuals or individuals who will be eligible for Medicaid who are seeking care in nursing facilities prior to placement. If you apply for such services there will be an initial evaluation to determine your eligibility, then an assessment of your need for care in such a facility and of your formal and informal support systems, along with preparation of an initial care plan and arrangement of or referral to needed services.

The Nursing Home Preadmission Screening Program is administered by the Division of Senior Affairs, Long-Term Care Options of the Department of Health and Senior Services. You may write to the division at CN-712, Trenton, NJ 08625-0712, or call (609) 588-2611.

II. HEALTH CARE

Recent advances in medical care have played a big role in extending our lives. But we have also begun to ask questions about the quality of life we expect. Making choices about health care gives you the power to exercise greater control over how you live. When you approach the end of life, the need for nursing home care requires that you learn about residential care facilities and means of paying for your care or, in appropriate cases, receiving hospice care.

This section addresses access to health care, health insurance, ensuring the quality of the health care you receive, HMOs, nursing homes, and long-term care. Questions addressed in these chapters include the following:

- If I want to die at home, can I get the care I need paid for by Medicare?
- Can I refuse treatment my doctor recommends? If I want to end my life, can I ask my doctor to help me?
- What insurance am I eligible for, and what will it cover?
- Can I get health care services at home?
- How do I go about finding a nursing home?
- What should I look for when I visit? Can I get help paying for a nursing home?
- What about help paying for home health care so I won't have to go to a nursing home?

4. Health Care, Health Insurance, and HMOs

MAKING HEALTH CARE CHOICES

You control the health care you receive by choosing the type of treatment you will accept and exercising your right to refuse treatment you do not want. It helps to understand your rights with regard to refusing treatment and to take advantage of the flexibility Medicare gives patients to choose hospice care when it is appropriate.

HOSPICE CARE

Victor has cancer, and the doctor has said that his condition is terminal. His wife is unable to provide all the care he requires, but he does not want to die in a hospital.

Victor may be eligible for hospice care, which will enable him to receive coordinated care from a team of professionals, provide support for his wife and family, and provide all of this care either in his home or in a separate facility so that he will not be subjected to the intensive and sometimes invasive care of a hospital. His care will be paid for by Medicare, including the supportive services and services provided at his home.

UNDERSTANDING THE LAW. *Hospice* is a term used to mean care provided for the patient's comfort when there is no prospect of improvement. Hospice care is provided in different settings—at home, in a separate facility, or in a hospital—depending on your wishes, the availability of family and friends to help with your care, and the programs available in your area.

In order to receive Medicare hospice benefits you must be enrolled in Medicare Part A and your doctor must determine that you have six months or less to live. To receive Medicare reimbursement for hospice care the care must be provided by an interdisciplinary team including at least one physician, one registered nurse, a social worker, and a spiritual counselor. This team will develop a care plan for you after making an evaluation of what will be needed. Medicare will cover the costs of care as well as the costs of home health aides, homemaker services, and inpatient treatment when required. In addition, Medicare will cover medical equipment, such as a hospital bed for your home.

TERMINATION OF CARE. One goal of this book is to provide you with information to enable you to receive and pay for the health care you choose. But a second issue is to enable you to maintain your autonomy and make your own choices at the end of your life, to the extent possible. You have the right to control your health care, including the right to refuse treatment. It is not enough that something might be helpful to you; you have to be willing to be treated. It is important to understand your right to refuse medical treatment and to consider the circumstances that would lead you to choose to refuse further treatment.

Chapter 8 discusses advance medical directives. These documents allow you to direct your doctor and your family with regard to making medical decisions for you when you are no longer able to express your wishes for yourself. Carefully consider whether you want to prepare these documents and what you want to say in them; it is much easier to make good decisions when you are not facing an immediate crisis. By thinking ahead of time about how you would like to be treated, you will be giving your health care providers and your family information based on well-thought-out opinions about how you would decide for yourself in various circumstances. If they are left guessing about what you would want, they are likely to make decisions that are different from those you would make for yourself.

If you are capable of expressing your own wishes, you will always have the right to decide which treatments you wish to receive and which you will refuse. You are legally entitled to understand what your doctor is recommending and to know the possible consequences of a given decision. For example, if your doctor advises you to consider surgery, you are entitled to know the likely outcome of the surgery and the possible risks. You should ask questions and be certain you understand the answers before making a decision, and you should not let anyone intimidate you into agreeing to something you are not sure you want.

ASSISTED SUICIDE. Although you have a right to refuse medical treatment you do not want to receive, you do not have the right to ask anyone for help in ending your life. When you sign an advance directive for health care (a living will), as discussed in chapter 8, you exercise the right to refuse unwanted treatment even when you are not able to discuss it with your doctor and have decided to refuse treatment. But you do not have the right to ask someone to help you end your life.

A great deal of attention has been paid to the issue of assisted suicide, particularly through the news coverage of Dr. Jack Kevorkian's efforts to help people who choose to end their lives. For some people with terminal illnesses the ability to receive assistance when they want to end their lives is important. If they want lethal doses of medication or require someone's physical assistance to end their lives, they need assistance or the cooperation of a doctor. But it is not legal for a doctor to prescribe medication with the purpose of allowing you to take a fatal dose, nor is it legal for someone to administer medication or take other steps that will bring your life to an end. New Jersey law prohibits assisted suicide. The law states that "A person who purposely aids another to commit suicide is guilty of a crime" (N.J.S.A. 2C:11–6). A crime has been committed even if there is no suicide, as it is also a crime to assist with an attempted suicide.

The United States Supreme Court recently considered the issue of whether we have a constitutional right to have someone assist us if we want to end our lives. The court was asked to decide whether assisted suicide is a logical extension of our right to determine our own medical treatment. The court decided that the U.S. Constitution provides no right to assisted suicide. As a result of this decision, the assisted suicide question can be decided separately by each state. Oregon is the first state with an assisted suicide law on the books. This law makes it permissible for a doctor to prescribe medication in a dose the doctor knows will be fatal to a patient the doctor knows intends to end his or her life. The actions of doctors and patients in Oregon will be closely watched by advocates for and against the right to assisted suicide. But for now the law in New Jersey remains unchanged.

PAYING FOR HEALTH CARE

Determining what health care you want to receive is one thing; paying for it is another. Most New Jersey residents are eligible for one or more forms of insurance to pay for their health care after retirement. Most people are aware of the Medicare and Medicaid programs, but do not fully understand what will be covered and what requirements must be met to receive benefits. For a detailed description of what Medicare covers and when Medicaid is available, read chapter 2.

If you are still working, you are probably provided with health insurance by your employer. You should understand how this insurance works and what it covers. Your employer will provide you with a summary of the plan that gives you the details of what is covered and what is excluded. If you leave your job you have some rights to maintain your insurance under state and federal law. Under the Consolidated Omnibus Reconciliation Act of 1985 (COBRA), you can buy into your existing health plan. You will have to pay for this coverage, but you are entitled to remain in the group you have been in while in the job and to pay the group rate your employer has been paying.

If you have been covered by your spouse's health insurance and he or she becomes eligible for Medicare before you do, you have the right to continue coverage under the plan of your spouse's employer. If your spouse is older than you are and therefore is covered by Medicare and leaves the employer's plan before you are old enough to receive Medicare, you can buy continuation coverage from your spouse's employer under COBRA.

MANAGED CARE PLANS. *Managed care* is the term used to describe the new developments in health care coverage. Whereas we traditionally received health insurance from a company or the government and health care from a hospital or doctor, now our insurance and our health care are essentially provided by a single entity. By limiting the doctors and hospitals we can use to those with which the managed care company has a contractual relationship, the company can limit its costs.

When you join an HMO (health maintenance organization) or other managed care plan, you give up some choice as to who will provide your care. In exchange you receive more comprehensive care, because coverage for routine preventive care is included in the plan.

If you are entitled to Medicare or Medicaid benefits, under the new Medicare+Choice program (discussed in chapter 2) you have the option of joining an HMO. In exchange for your premiums, if any, you will receive the full range of coverage. For Medicare patients an HMO should eliminate the need for Medigap insurance. Consider carefully whether this option is for you. The range of services you can obtain through an HMO may be useful, and that can be a deciding factor. But if the restrictions on doctors or the geographic area covered limits you from receiving all the care you require, an HMO may not be for you.

It is important to note that an insurance company that is offering an HMO can change its mind and abandon a Medicare HMO. This has happened several times; companies have made business decisions to halt HMO services. If this occurs, you always have the option to go back to traditional Medicare, although your choices for Medigap insurance may be more expensive. The law will protect your right to purchase certain Medigap policies in this circumstance, so you can be assured a policy will be available even if your health is poor. You can also transfer to another HMO if one is available in your area. Pay attention to the information you receive, and contact Medicare if you have any questions.

Legislation that is being considered in Congress would create a "patients' bill of rights" to ensure that patients in HMOs have the right to appeal if they are denied care and that they have access to any specialists they need. Although this bill of rights may not become law, the Department of Health and Human Services is including the principles involved in regulations that cover Medicaid.

HOME HEALTH CARE. If you have been in the hospital or have a chronic condition that requires nursing services but want to continue living at home, home health care services may meet your needs and eliminate or delay the need to move to a nursing home. Today it is possible to receive many medical services at home. You will have to find appropriate care and locate funding for it. To determine whether home care will meet your needs, you will have to learn the answers to the following questions:

- What kind of services do I need in order to stay at home?
- Can I expect to live safely at home if these services are provided?
- Can I afford to pay for these services myself?
- Are these services covered by any programs for which I am eligible?
- How do I obtain services from such programs?
- Who provides the types of services I need?

Home health care services can range from full-time nursing services to regular visits for monitoring and treatment. Services may also include assistance with basic activities of daily living (ADL) such as bathing and dressing. But limited coverage of such services by

Medicare and Medicaid makes it important to determine if the services you need will be paid for by these programs. Medicare, in particular, limits access to home health care benefits. Even when services are covered, you should expect to have to advocate for the extent of services you need. If you have employer-sponsored health insurance, check to see if home health care services are covered.

Many companies in New Jersey provide home health care services. Before making any agreements with a company, ask questions about what you can expect. The following are some areas to ask about:

- Is the company certified by Medicare and Medicaid? Unless a company is certified, these programs will not pay for services.
- Is the company licensed? Is it accredited? Licensing and accreditation will vary depending on the services offered, but they provide an indication that a company meets relevant standards.
- What are the qualifications of the staff? Make sure that the staff members who will be providing services to you have training and experience relevant to your needs.
- How are grievances handled?
- How are services provided? Will I be involved in planning my care? What backup services are available? Are services available twenty-four hours a day, seven days a week? When can service begin?
- How is billing handled?
- What is the company's reputation? Ask for references, and call them. Ask about the company in your community, or ask hospital social work staff members about it. Find out how often the references make referrals to the company and what feedback they have received from patients.

One way to find an appropriate provider is to ask friends and family members to recommend companies that have provided them with good care.

5. Nursing Homes and Long-Term Care

When the need for long-term care arises, most people think first of nursing homes. But other options are available. What is right for you will depend on the level of care you require, whether you have family available to provide care at home, what you can afford to pay for yourself, and what services are available in your community. Other options to consider include home health care, respite care, adult day care, and assisted living. This chapter looks specifically at nursing homes and more generally at funding available for home health care. Assisted living is addressed in chapter 19. For information on other options, contact your county Office on Aging (see appendix A).

NURSING HOME SELECTION AND EVALUATION

Dolly was hospitalized after she fell and broke her hip. Surgery to repair her hip led to a mild stroke that has left her unable to care for herself or to make decisions about where she will live. Her doctor has told Dolly's family that she will not be able to return home for some time; she will continue to require skilled nursing and rehabilitation services. The doctor has advised her family to locate a nursing home where Dolly can live. The doctor cannot tell them whether she will ever be able to live at home again. They have been told that she will be released from the hospital in less than a week, so they need to go about finding a nursing home promptly. They understand that Medicare will pay for her care for about three weeks.

Dolly has given power of attorney to her son, but has never put his name on her bank accounts or added his name to the deed to her house. All her property is owned solely by her. Her children are afraid that putting her in a nursing home will require turning over all of her assets and selling her house. None of her children live near to her, and they are very concerned about how they will locate a nursing home before she is released from the hospital.

The first concern of Dolly's family, that all of her assets will have to be turned over to a nursing home to secure her admission, reflects a common misunderstanding about nursing homes. Nursing homes

---

RESOURCES TO HELP YOU FIND A NURSING HOME

The Division of Licensing and Evaluation of the New Jersey Department of Health and Senior Services offers a booklet entitled *Selecting a Long-Term Care Facility: A Guide for New Jersey Consumers*, which includes general information and lists area facilities by county. For a copy call (800) 367-6543 or (609) 588-7771.

---

provide services under contract and are paid at a set rate. If an individual can afford to pay for the services, the patient pays. If the patient has exhausted his or her assets, Medicaid often pays for nursing home services. In some circumstances Medicare will pay for a nursing home. In Dolly's case, Medicare will pay for several weeks of care in a nursing home. But a nursing home will not take over all of Dolly's assets.

It seems that Dolly's family has confused a nursing home with a type of life care community. Some life care communities require that all assets be turned over to them in exchange for a promise of lifetime care. This type of arrangement usually includes the provision of assisted living before the person needs nursing home care, along with whatever degree of care is needed during the remainder of the resident's life. Other types of continuing care communities provide this range of services but do not require that all assets be turned over to them. More information on various types of housing is available in chapter 19.

Dolly's family should examine the contract any nursing home requests that they sign. Since Medicare will pay for Dolly's care upon her admission, the nursing home is not permitted to demand a deposit or advance payment. If her stay were not to be covered by Medicare, requesting a reasonable deposit would be allowed. It is also not permissible to require an agreement that Dolly will not apply for Medicaid for a given period of time. When she becomes financially eligible she must be able to apply for benefits. Dolly's family should not be requested to guarantee payments for her. If the contract requires a guarantee from a third party, the family should refuse to sign.

The hospital social worker should be able to assist Dolly's family with finding possible nursing homes. The burden will be on the family to visit the facilities available and decide which they prefer. They should review the next section regarding what to consider and should check with the New Jersey Division of Licensing and Evaluation for a list of facilities in the area where Dolly lives. The division can provide them with information about complaints against a facility so they can learn of any reported problems.

WHAT TO CONSIDER WHEN SELECTING A NURSING HOME. Remember that any nursing home you select, whether for yourself or for a family member, will provide care and housing for the time it is necessary. Given the variety of choices available, it is important to look at more than one nursing home before deciding which will be the best choice. You are choosing both a residence and a care provider, so think about the criteria on which you will rely to make your decision.

Consider the medical services that are offered. Ask questions about what staffing is available in the building at all times and whether other medical professionals are on call. Since nursing care is primary, look for a facility with licensed nurses on duty and doctors on call. Find out how often other services, such as speech and physical therapy, are offered and what credentials the providers have.

A significant question to ask is how physical or chemical restraints are used. Historically some nursing homes have used drugs or physical restraints to keep residents under control. Either they have been used without doctors' orders or orders have been written to allow the use of restraints "as needed." Federal law now restricts the use of restraints; they must be used only for emergencies or under specific doctors' orders. Doctors should authorize their use only when residents may harm themselves. Even when they are used, they should be used for a limited time. Ask about a nursing home's policy on the use of restraints, and observe how residents are treated by the staff.

The physical facility is also important. Is the building clean and in good repair? Can residents go outside? Are rooms pleasantly furnished, and do residents have a place to keep personal property?

Most important is the general impression you develop. What you observe about interactions between residents and staff members will give you an idea of the character of the facility. If the staff seems unresponsive to residents, there is no reason to think your needs will be met promptly. Consider what activities are offered and whether the residents seem to be able to participate in activities they enjoy. Also think about provisions for receiving visits and convenience for visitors.

IF THERE ARE PROBLEMS AT A NURSING HOME

If you have a complaint about a nursing home, first see if you can resolve it through the facility's grievance process. Document your complaint, and ask the administration to respond.

If your problems are not resolved and you feel you are not getting services to which you are entitled, you may file a complaint with the Division of Licensing and Certification of the New Jersey Department of Health and Senior Services at CN-367, Trenton, NJ 08625-0367, or call (800) 792-9770.

If your complaint concerns the mistreatment of a patient, contact the Ombudsman for the Institutionalized Elderly at 101 South Broad Street, CN-808, Trenton, NJ 08625-0808, or call (800) 792-8820 or (609) 292-8016.

Can your family reach you easily, and are the visiting hours convenient? Overall, you will want to find a safe, clean facility that will meet your needs in as pleasant an environment as possible. It will help to compare several nursing homes in order to get a sense of different possibilities.

THE NURSING HOME RESIDENTS' BILL OF RIGHTS. Since the federal government funds a significant percentage of nursing home care through Medicare and Medicaid, the government has also taken an interest in the quality of the care being provided. In response to concerns about abuses by some nursing homes, federal law now requires all nursing homes that are certified to accept Medicare or Medicaid to follow a Nursing Home Residents' Bill of Rights. The issues covered by this law are worth considering as you evaluate a nursing home.

The issues covered by the Nursing Home Residents' Bill of Rights include the following:

- The right to be informed of your rights, to air your grievances, and not to suffer retaliation.
- The right to have reasonable access to members of your family, friends, and advocates.

- The right to receive clear information about the services that will be provided and the charges for those services.
- The right to receive complete information about your medical condition; to participate in planning about your treatment, including the right to refuse treatment; and to choose your own doctor.
- The right to make decisions about your finances or choose who you want to make financial decisions for you.
- The right to privacy, dignity, and respect, including the right to be free from physical or mental abuse and the excessive use of restraints.
- The right to be discharged or transferred only for medical reasons, and the right to receive written notice of transfers.

PAYING FOR LONG-TERM CARE

Figuring out how to pay for a nursing home or other type of long-term care is essential. In New Jersey the average monthly cost of a nursing home is officially estimated to be at least $3,376 but is generally believed to be much higher. It is easy to spend $100,000 per year on nursing home care or home health care. So using up your life's savings is not impossible or even unlikely. This reality is what has led to the development of an area of elder law known as Medicaid planning, whose purpose is assisting seniors with redistributing, retitling, or disposing of assets so that property can be preserved for a noninstitutionalized spouse or passed on to children before everything is spent on long-term care.

Although Medicaid is available to those who are impoverished by the need to pay for nursing home care, Congress has made it clear that the sophisticated planning that allows seniors to pass the bulk of their assets to the next generation while using Medicaid to fund their own care is disfavored. Congress has twice attempted to make this practice difficult or impossible. First a law was passed that made it illegal for a person to make any financial transfers in order to create Medicaid eligibility. When that law proved extremely unpopular (it was referred to as the Granny Goes to Jail Law), it was modified to make it illegal to counsel someone to become eligible (thus sending the lawyer rather than "granny" to jail).

Although it may not be desirable or possible to make yourself eligible for Medicaid if your assets are substantial, it is still worth considering the following information so you can maintain all the resources to which you are entitled. This is particularly true if you have a spouse, partner, or child who is dependent on the same resources. Congress does not want you to take steps to make yourself eligible for Medicaid. But taking steps to take care of your family is reasonable, even if it has the result of making you eligible for Medicaid.

A NOTE FOR GAY AND LESBIAN SENIORS. You will find that much of the law is written to accommodate married couples, and it makes many assumptions about what married couples require as they age and after death. Since these protections are not available if you and your partner are not legally married to each other, no matter how long your relationship, it is important that you understand the choices available and plan ahead so that your partner will be cared for as you wish. The assumptions in the law make it easier for a married person to feel that his or her spouse will be cared for even if they do not do any planning. But if you plan ahead you can be assured that some or all of the same protections will be available to you and your partner.

Medicaid makes provisions for a noninstitutionalized spouse when one partner in a marriage requires nursing home care. There are no similar provisions for an unmarried couple, so planning for long-term care is essential. Dividing assets that are joint and considering the value of private alternatives such as long-term care insurance may be necessary for you.

OPTIONS FOR LONG-TERM CARE. Medicaid is not the only payment source for long-term care, and you should certainly consider other sources. Although nursing homes are not supposed to discriminate against Medicaid recipients, many prefer at least some period of payment prior to relying on Medicaid, so ensuring that assets are available for six months or more will provide you with a greater choice of facilities. In addition to relying on Medicaid, long-term care is generally funded in one of the following ways: private pay, or paying for yourself; long-term care insurance; Medicare, in those circumstances covered by the Medicare regulations; and veterans' benefits.

If you have substantial assets, you can plan to pay for your own long-term care either at home or in a nursing home. But you might want to consider purchasing long-term care insurance if you want to protect assets or you are not certain your assets will be sufficient.

Long-term care or nursing home insurance is quite expensive, so it may not be a realistic option for everyone. Since your age and health are significant factors in determining the premiums for this insurance, it is less expensive if you buy it when you are relatively young and healthy, perhaps when you are in your late fifties. Do not wait until the need is obvious before you look into this possibility.

As with any investment, make sure you understand what you can expect when you purchase long-term care insurance. First, you want to know that the company will still be in business when you begin making claims, so check on its financial stability. Insurance companies are rated by several different services, and you can find these ratings in your library.

If the company is sound, find out what the policy will cover and what must happen for you to receive benefits. Are there exclusions for certain conditions, such as Alzheimer's disease? Avoid such a policy. How much is the benefit you will receive? If the benefit is $100 per day and the actual cost of your care is $175 per day, you must be sure you will be able to make up the difference. Is there a number of days you must pay before coverage begins? Different policies set different deductible periods. Will the benefit increase over time? Make sure there is an inflation provision so that as nursing home costs increase, your benefit will increase, too.

How long will you receive benefits? Your premiums will vary depending on the term of coverage. Since it is impossible to predict the future, you would do well to buy the longest-term insurance you can afford. When you apply for Medicaid, the government will evaluate your financial transactions during the years prior to your application. This "look-back" period for Medicaid is now three years, so if transfers are made at the time you enter a nursing home that would affect your eligibility, you will want insurance to pay for three years. But future changes to Medicare rules could affect this strategy. Congress could extend the look-back period in order to limit who receives Medicaid.

Are preexisting conditions excluded? If so, find out if this practice will affect you. What will have to happen for benefits to begin? Different polices use different measures. You might need a doctor's certification that nursing home care is necessary, or it could be enough that you cannot perform several "activities of daily living" such as bathing, dressing, and feeding yourself. The policy may provide that cognitive impairment, certified by a physician, will trigger benefits. You should understand which of these will be true for a policy you purchase.

A policy that covers home health care benefits may make it possible for you to stay at home instead of in a nursing home and still receive care. Ask about such benefits, and be sure you are getting the coverage you want. Premiums will vary depending on your age and the coverage you select. Once you have long-term care insurance, you want it to be guaranteed renewable so that as long as you pay the premiums the company cannot cancel your policy. Ask questions until you feel that you know what you are paying for, and make sure all guarantees or assurances are included in the written policy documents.

If the cost of long-term care insurance is prohibitive or you need to find other sources of funds to pay for nursing home care, consider whether you have assets that could be used to generate cash. One example is cashing in your life insurance. It also might be possible to use a reverse mortgage to pay for care (see chapter 17). Often a life insurance policy will have a living benefits rider that will allow you to receive a percentage of the death benefit when there has been a triggering event, such as diagnosis of a terminal illness or the need for long-term care. The requirements and the percentage of the total value that you will receive are spelled out in the terms of the policy itself.

If you do not have a living benefits rider to your life insurance policy, you might be able to use a viatical settlement to obtain cash for your policy. A viatical settlement involves selling your life insurance to an investor in order to obtain a percentage of its value. The investor pays you and then continues to pay the premiums until your death. After your death the investor receives the benefits. The amount you receive is based on your life expectancy. These settlements are generally used only when life expectancy is under two years. The money you receive from living benefits and viatical settlements is largely exempt from federal taxes but, at least at present, are probably subject to New Jersey state taxes.

Viatical settlements are a relatively new idea, and although they are regulated in some states, there is no New Jersey regulation of the investors. Make sure you shop around and understand any agreements you sign. It is important to consider that after buying your life insurance the investor will want to keep track of your health. This means that you will probably have to provide access to your medical records. But if you feel comfortable with this your life insurance may provide you with access to cash at a time when you most need it.

FOR MORE INFORMATION
ON VETERANS' BENEFITS

If you think you might be entitled to long-term care as a veteran
or as a veteran's family member, call the United States Veterans
Administration at (202) 273-5400 or the New Jersey Veterans
Administration at (609) 530-6957.

VETERANS' BENEFITS. If you or your spouse is a veteran of the United
States armed services, you may be able to obtain long-term care through
the Veterans Administration (VA). The VA runs its own nursing homes,
and in some cases will also provide benefits in a private nursing home.
Veterans with service-related disabilities receive free care. If you do not
have a service-related disability, the VA will provide care if you are unable
to afford it. The VA has its own criteria that are applied to determine
eligibility. New Jersey provides care in an old soldiers' home for New
Jersey veterans and their families. Depending on space availability, care
is provided for a veteran honorably discharged who has been a New Jersey
resident for at least two years prior to the date of application or who was
a New Jersey resident at the time of entrance into active military service.
Spouses, surviving spouses, and parents of veterans are admitted if they
meet certain specific criteria and a place is available.

MEDICARE COVERAGE FOR NURSING HOME CARE. Medicare covers
nursing home care under some limited circumstances. The requirements are that the need for nursing home care must follow a hospital
stay of at least three days and must come within thirty days of discharge
from the hospital. The patient must need skilled nursing care as
opposed to custodial care. Skilled nursing care must be ordered by a
physician and must be carried out by a nurse or other skilled professional. In the story of Dolly, discussed earlier, Dolly has had surgery,
and afterward she needs to receive round-the-clock nursing care.
Therefore, her doctor is recommending nursing home care, and Medicare will pay for a period of time. If Dolly stops making progress under
the skilled nursing care plan, the Medicare payments may stop. They
are intended to cover only skilled care in a certified facility, so if it is

found that the patient needs only custodial care, Medicare will stop paying. But the difference between skilled and custodial care can be difficult to determine. For example, even if Dolly will not get better but is receiving physical therapy to prevent deterioration, her therapy may be considered skilled nursing care, since it is administered by a physical therapist. If you disagree with a decision that the patient no longer needs skilled care, you have the right to appeal. See chapter 2 for more information on appealing Medicare denials.

If skilled nursing care is required and the patient is making progress, Medicare will pay 100 percent of the cost for 20 days. After twenty days the patient is responsible for $95 per day and Medicare will pay the balance for the next 80 days. Many Medigap insurance policies cover the patient's portion of the cost, depending on which plan the patient has. After 100 days of care, Medicare will no longer provide coverage.

MEDICARE COVERAGE FOR HOME HEALTH CARE. Medicare will pay for some health services to be provided in your home if you qualify. You must have been hospitalized for three days and still need skilled nursing care or therapy, and you must not be able to leave the house to receive services. This coverage is intended to allow patients to remain at home with the services they require when the full extent of nursing home care is not required, but it can be difficult to get Medicare to cover home health services for more than a few hours a week. Depending on what is needed, this may not be enough for you to remain at home.

If Medicare is available for home health care services, it can also cover some custodial care services, such as assistance with bathing. A prior hospitalization is not required. Services must be provided by a Medicare-certified home health care agency. The agency will visit you and determine what services it thinks will be covered by Medicare. If the agency does not think the services you need will be covered, the only way to appeal is to demand that the agency bill Medicare. If Medicare does not ultimately pay, you will have to pay for the services you receive. But reversal on appeal is not unusual, and if you do not get the service you will have nothing to appeal.

FINANCIAL ELIGIBILITY FOR MEDICAID

Dolly, described in the story above, will be transferred from the hospital to a nursing home, and initially Medicare will pay for her care.

But if she continues to need nursing home care after Medicare runs out, she may be eligible for Medicaid coverage. In order to determine whether she can receive Medicaid payments, an evaluation will be made of her income and her resources.

To qualify for Medicaid in New Jersey, Dolly must be a U.S. citizen and a resident of New Jersey. She must be over age sixty-five or must be blind or disabled. If her income is below the current limit ($1,482 per month at this writing, adjusted annually) and she has no more than $2,000 in assets, she can qualify for the Medicaid Only program. If her income is higher but her assets are only $4,000, she can qualify for the medically needy program (see chapter 3), which will not provide as many benefits but will cover all or part of the cost of nursing home care.

The assets that will be counted toward the resource limits for Dolly's Medicaid eligibility include everything except certain specific items, such as her car, personal effects, and life insurance with a face value of $1,500 or less. If property is held in an irrevocable trust or is otherwise unavailable to her, it will not be counted.

If Dolly made transfers of property before her hospitalization, Medicaid will look at these transfers and determine if she should be penalized. For example, if she owned rental property and she transferred ownership to her son six months before applying for benefits, Medicaid will determine the market value of the property and penalize her by denying payment for the number of months that sale of the property would presumably have allowed her to pay for herself. If the property was worth $100,000, Medicaid will divide that by the average monthly cost of a nursing home (currently $3,376), resulting in a twenty-nine–month penalty. For twenty-nine months Dolly will not receive Medicaid payments, even if the property is no longer available to her. If, on the other hand, the transfer was made more than thirty-six months ago or it was for value (to pay off debt, for example) it will not be counted against her.

RECOVERY BY THE STATE. The state of New Jersey attempts to recover money spent on nursing home care from the estate of deceased Medicaid recipients. If there is a surviving spouse, recovery will be postponed until the spouse's death. If the recipient owned property, the state will put a lien on the property unless it is occupied by the spouse or an exempt child or sibling.

WARNING

When you apply for Medicaid you must swear that you have accurately stated all of your assets and income. Medicaid will request copies of supporting documents such as bank statements and tax returns. **Failing to report all of your assets is a crime.**

Bill was recently diagnosed with Alzheimer's disease, which is still at an early stage. Among other things, his doctor has told him that although he can expect to live comfortably at home for some time, he should assume that he will probably need to be cared for in a nursing home in the future. Bill and his wife have some assets, but not enough to pay for extended nursing home care and still support Bill's wife. Bill wants to be sure his wife will have enough money, and he also wants her to be able to stay in their home as long as she wants.

Bill and his wife have the opportunity to prepare for the likelihood of his needing nursing home care. With planning they can make the best use of their assets so that Bill's wife will have some income and can stay in their home. Depending on the extent of their assets, at some point Bill will probably become eligible for Medicaid to cover his nursing home costs. But how many of the couple's own assets will be spent on his care will depend, in part, on what they do now. The law allows a certain level of income and certain property to be retained by the spouse who is not institutionalized. By planning to make certain purchases and maximize the allowable expenses, they can provide for Bill's wife's needs without running into trouble with the Medicaid law.

UNDERSTANDING THE LAW. Some people expect the government to pay for nursing home care, and they want to be able to preserve their property for their spouse and children to use and to inherit. Medicaid is intended to be a payer of last resort, covering care for those who cannot afford to pay for themselves. But provisions are made in the law for the spouse who remains in the community to have continuing income and for people like Bill and his wife to keep some assets. This is a complicated area of the law, and it is advisable that you consult an

FINDING AN ELDER LAW ATTORNEY

Some attorneys have chosen to specialize in the field of elder law in order to develop special expertise in dealing with problems such as Medicaid eligibility. One way to find an attorney with this experience is to write the National Academy of Elder Law Attorneys (NAELA) at 1604 N. Country Club Road, Tucson, AZ 85716, or call (520) 881-4005 (web site: www.naela.org). The organization sells referral directories of member attorneys in this area. NAELA also certifies attorneys who meet certain standards and who have passed an exam proving their expertise in elder law. If your attorney is a certified elder law attorney (CELA), you can be confident he or she has met these standards.

attorney before making transfers. An elder law attorney can assist you in determining what is and is not permissible so that you will not be penalized by Medicaid. The following paragraphs review the general provisions of the law, but this is a very complex issue and the law changes frequently. Do not rely on this information alone.

What Bill and his wife should understand about using Medicaid to pay for nursing home care is that if they have income and assets above a certain level, they will have to pay for care themselves. But because Medicaid has some exemptions, some purchases and transfers of assets are permitted and will allow them to have more control over how their money is spent. Transferring assets in other ways can lead to Medicaid penalties, so planning ahead and paying attention to what is allowed makes a big difference.

When applying for Medicaid it is important to include information about all of your assets, but not all assets will be counted in determining eligibility. You should also understand that Medicaid will look at the income and assets of both you and your spouse. When making changes in how property is titled or when making gifts to family members, it helps to understand how Medicaid will view the actions you have taken.

EXEMPT ASSETS. These are assets that the Medicaid law allows you to keep. You can be eligible if you have no more than $2,000—$4,000 if

HOME OWNERSHIP TRANSFERS

If you transfer ownership of your house, it can be transferred without penalty only to one of the following:

- Your spouse
- Your minor, blind, or disabled child
- Your child who has lived with you for two years, whose care for you prevented the need for nursing home care
- Your sibling who has lived in the house for one year prior to your move to a nursing home and who has an equity interest.

you are medically needy (see chapter 3)—plus a burial fund of $1,500, a car of any value, and a certain amount of personal property including jewelry, clothing, and your home. Your home is exempt as long as you, your spouse, or your minor, blind, or disabled child lives there.

INCOME FOR THE COMMUNITY SPOUSE. Medicaid law acknowledges that if one spouse is institutionalized the other spouse will still need income to live on. If all of the couple's assets are counted without making allowance for the community spouse's needs, the healthy spouse will have little or nothing to live on. So the law determines what is known as the "community spouse resource allowance." This will allow Bill's wife to keep half of the couple's assets up to a maximum amount that is changed each year ($81,960 at present). In addition, income that comes directly to her, such as a pension check in her name or income from an annuity, will not be counted in determining Bill's income. If the income is in both her name and Bill's, half will be counted as Bill's income. His wife is entitled to a certain minimum income, which is also adjusted each year (currently $2,049 per month). If her income is below this amount, she will be entitled to enough of Bill's income to bring her up to this level before the money goes to pay his expenses.

In 1998 the New Jersey Supreme Court decided that an individual retirement account (IRA) in the name of one spouse is to be considered available for the support of the other spouse. This changed the previous interpretation of the law, so if you were previously told that you could hold money in an IRA and not count that amount when determining

---

PENALTY PERIODS FOR TRANSFERS

Note that the rules about penalty periods for transfers do not apply if a transfer is made to your spouse, your blind or disabled child, your caretaker child, or your sibling who meets certain conditions.

Medicaid eligibility, that is no longer true. The money could instead be used to purchase an annuity, which would be considered part of your income when determining eligibility.

CONVERTING OR TRANSFERRING ASSETS. Once the calculations have been made as to what resources Bill can keep and what his wife can keep, they are expected to spend the balance of their assets. The money can be used to pay for nursing home care, or it can be used for other legitimate purposes before it goes to pay for care. For example, paying off debts or making home improvements is considered a valid use of assets. It might make more sense for Bill and his wife to sell their house and purchase a new, more expensive home. They could prepay for a funeral. By putting money in an irrevocable funeral trust they can ensure that funds will be available for this purpose, and they will not be counted as an asset. (Before taking this step yourself, read chapter 16 on funeral fraud.) If they create an irrevocable Medicaid funeral trust for Bill, they can fund this trust with whatever amount of money they wish to put aside for his funeral. It must be done when they anticipate that within six months Bill will apply for Medicaid.

If Bill's wife purchases an annuity for her own benefit before Bill must move into a nursing home, the annuity will not be counted for Medicaid purposes. If, on the other hand, she has an IRA, it will be considered a "countable" asset that could help pay for Bill's care. Entering a continuing care retirement community might also be an option for the couple, which would provide for lifetime care for both of them. Bill's diagnosis may exclude them from some choices; often one must be healthy to enter a continuing care community. If this option is available, the cost would be considered the value of the services provided, and therefore it would not be seen as an invalid

TRUSTS

A trust is a legal structure that owns whatever property is placed in trust. Only the trustees of the trust can make decisions about how trust property will be spent, so you may use it to make money available to you though it is not actually owned by you. Special tax and Medicaid rules apply to trusts, so be sure you understand what is being done and what it will mean for you if you are the creator or the beneficiary of a trust. Because trusts have been used to protect assets, Medicaid will look at transfers made to a trust as much as five years before an application for benefits. Trusts can be useful, but be sure you understand their implications.

transfer. For more information on continuing care retirement communities, see chapter 19.

Since it will probably be several years before Bill requires the full-time care of a nursing home, he and his wife may want to make some transfers of property before applying for Medicaid. If they choose to take this step, they should consult with an elder law attorney to ensure that they follow the current law and do not create problems for themselves.

As has been said, Medicaid will consider any transactions that have been made within three years of the date of application. If Bill requires nursing home care within three years of making transfers, he and his wife should be certain to have enough money available to pay for his care until the three years have passed. If property is placed in trust there is a five-year "look-back" period for these transfers. In addition, gifts have tax consequences that should be considered. Finally, once Bill and his wife have transferred property, it will no longer be available to them. If they give it to one of their children, for example, and the child is later divorced, the property may become part of a divorce settlement. It is important to know and consider all of the possible ramifications before making transfers of this type. If property is transferred to a trust (see box, this page), there may be additional consequences, and expert advice should be obtained.

III. PERSONAL DECISION MAKING

As we get older we face the prospect of losing the ability to care for ourselves or to express our wishes because we are unconscious or incapacitated. Most people would prefer not to think about this prospect, but a little advance planning can give you the assurance that what you want is what will be done. This section discusses the various steps you can take to prepare for whatever may come with age.

The following chapters discuss wills, powers of attorney and alternative financial arrangements, advance directives, and guardianship and conservatorship. At the end of each chapter you will find examples of forms you can complete to express your wishes, with comments to help you understand how to customize the forms to meet your needs. With these documents completed you can be confident that those who care about you will be able to take care of your affairs as you wish, your wishes for medical treatment will be expressed to your doctors, and after death your estate will be distributed as you wish.

Some of the typical questions that are answered in this section are as follows:

- Do I have to leave my property to my children?
- Who is permitted to be my executor?
- Can I write my own will?
- How do I make changes to my will?
- Where is the best place to keep a will?
- Do wills get registered somewhere?
- Is a will that was executed in another state valid after I move to New Jersey?
- Is there a simple way to administer a small estate?
- I would like my daughter to be able to help me by writing checks to pay bills and otherwise taking care of what needs to be done when I am no longer able to do this for myself. How can I make sure she will be allowed to act for me?
- What are the benefits of a power of attorney?
- If I give a durable power of attorney to someone, can I be sure no one will be appointed my guardian?
- Can I revoke a power of attorney?
- Is a living will valid in New Jersey?

- How can I be sure a doctor or hospital will follow my wishes regarding medical care if I am unconscious?
- When is a guardianship necessary?
- What is the difference between guardianship and conservatorship?
- Can I object to the creation of a conservatorship?

6. Wills

WHY YOU NEED A WILL

William does not own very much, and he does not think he needs a will. His children and grandchildren occasionally mention that they like something, such as a portrait of his deceased wife, and he invariably says, "When I die, you can have it." He assumes that his children will get together after his death and decide who will take what.

Although a will might not be essential to William, it would still be advisable for him to make one. Even if the will does little more than appoint an executor, it will provide a structure for the children and grandchildren to use to divide up his property and resolve any disputes that arise. If particular items have been promised to various individuals, the will can list who is to receive what so that there will be no questions. Since writing a will does not have to be an expensive or difficult process, there is no reason for William not to provide this security for his family.

NAMING AN EXECUTOR. A will names an executor for your estate and provides instructions to the executor regarding what you want done with your property after your death. The executor is the person (or persons) you choose to take the steps necessary to follow your instructions and the law regarding probate of your will. The executor can be any adult, including someone who will receive property from your estate. It can be a member of your family, a friend, your lawyer, or a bank. What is important is that the person or institution you name be willing to do the work involved, since it can be a chore to do everything required.

If you do not have a will or do not name an executor, the person who takes responsibility for doing all this work may have to post a bond. This means that he or she will have to put up money to ensure that they will not use the money in your estate for his or her own use or in any way other than in accordance with your instructions and the law. By naming an executor you can choose the person you think is best for the job, and you can state that your executor should not have to post a bond.

The responsibilities of the executor will be to collect all of your property, pay any debts and taxes due, file tax returns, and distribute the remaining assets according to the instructions in your will. The executor may sue and be sued on behalf of the estate.

An executor is entitled to a fee for his or her services. If you appoint a family member or friend to serve as executor, he or she may decide whether to take a fee. If you appoint a bank or your lawyer to be executor, this institution or individual will take a fee. If the court appoints an administrator because you do not have a will and the administrator is not a member of your family, you can be certain that this person will choose to collect a fee. The fee is a percentage of the total estate, usually about 5 to 6 percent, depending on the size of the estate.

DISTRIBUTING YOUR PROPERTY. You may leave your property entirely to one person, or you may divide it in any way you choose. Your will controls the distribution of all "probate assets," meaning what you own, including your real estate, car, jewelry, and items of sentimental value. Things you own jointly with someone else or anything for which you have named a beneficiary, such as life insurance or a pension account, are considered "nonprobate assets," and they will pass directly to the surviving owner or beneficiary no matter what your will says. You cannot leave instructions about nonprobate assets in your will.

LEAVING FUNERAL INSTRUCTIONS. If you wish, you may include funeral instructions in your will. Note, however, that if you do this your executor will either need to know your wishes ahead of time or need to know where your will can be found at the time decisions must be made about your funeral. If no one reads your will until after your funeral, your instructions may not be followed.

WHAT WILL HAPPEN AFTER YOUR DEATH?

If you have signed a will, your executor will take the will to the Surrogate's Office in the county in which you reside, along with a death certificate and a check to cover the filing fees. This can be done once ten days have passed following the date of death. The surrogate will admit the will to probate and issue "letters testamentary," a document required by various agencies to prove that the executor is the person responsible for handling the estate. See

QUESTIONS TO ASK YOURSELF ABOUT YOUR WILL

- Does it distribute all the property you might own at the time of your death, even if you do not own it at the time of writing your will? (That is, if you win the lottery or someone leaves you a house, will it be included in your will?)
- Does it name an executor and an alternate?
- Does it reflect what you want done with your property, including family and friends you want to receive something and specifically excluding family members you choose not to include?
- Has it been signed, dated, and witnessed by two people, neither or whom will receive anything under the will?
- Will your executor know where to find the original of your will?

appendix D for the address and phone number of your county Surrogate's Office.

Admitting the will to probate will involve establishing that it is a valid will. If you have a will that follows one of the forms described elsewhere in this chapter, this should be a simple process. Attached to the will itself you will see a document called a self-proving affidavit. If you and the witnesses sign this affidavit before a notary or attorney, your will can be admitted to probate without the need for the witnesses to appear in court; the affidavit attached to the will will authenticate its validity.

IF YOU HAVE A SMALL ESTATE. If you die without a will, your estate is worth less than $5,000, and you have no surviving spouse, an heir will be entitled to distribute the assets of your estate without administration or posting a bond. A family member will obtain the written consent of your other heirs, if any, and then complete an affidavit with the Surrogate's Office of the county where you resided listing all of the assets of the estate and their value. The assets will be used to pay off any debts you have incurred and then will be distributed to your heirs. If you have a surviving spouse and your estate is worth less than

INTESTATE SUCCESSION

If you die without a will, the law requires that your estate be divided along the following lines, depending on who survives you and their degree of relationship to you (N.J.S.A. 3B:5-3 et seq.):

- To your spouse, children, and parents, if any are living
- If none of the preceding survives you, to your brothers and sisters or their children
- If none of the preceding survives you, to your grandparents
- If none of the preceding survives you, to your aunts, uncles, cousins, or other descendants of your grandparents
- If no other descendants of your grandparents survive you, to the state

$10,000, your spouse may follow this procedure and receive $5,000 of the estate, free of your debts. Once the affidavit is filed the person obtaining it will have the rights, powers, and duties of an administrator.

IF YOU DO NOT WRITE A WILL. If you die without writing a will (intestate), the Surrogate's Office will issue "letters of administration" instead of "letters testamentary." There is little practical difference between the role of an executor with letters testamentary and that of an administrator with letters of administration; the administrator must distribute the estate according to New Jersey statute. The law will decide who gets what. What you would have chosen or how the administrator thinks you would have liked your estate distributed will not be taken into consideration. This is known as "intestate succession" and can lead to distribution of your assets to individuals other than those you wanted to receive your property. For example, even if you want all of your property to go to your niece, if you have a brother some property will go to your brother.

WHEN YOU NEED A LAWYER

Ethel has written down her wishes as to how her money and property should be distributed after her death, and she has signed and dated the document at the end. She has written that her money should be divided among all of her children, with one child, Betty, receiving a larger share. She wants Betty to have more than the others because she was injured in a car accident and cannot work; Betty receives government disability benefits. Ethel has included in her will that Betty should live in her house until she is no longer able to keep up the property and then it should be sold and each of the children should receive an equal share of the proceeds of the house. She believes that by writing her wishes down she has provided for the needs of Betty, who needs extra help, without depriving any of her other children.

Ethel has written a valid will, which can be admitted to probate. But she may not have accomplished what she set out to do, since providing for Betty's needs might require a more sophisticated estate plan than the one she has devised on her own (see the section entitled "Providing for Children with Disabilities"). By leaving money to Betty she may cause Betty to lose government benefits until the money is spent, so in the end she will have less than the other children, not more. Ethel also has not appointed an executor in her will, so she has lost the opportunity to tell the court who she would like to serve in this role and to ensure that her executor does not need to post a bond.

Most lawyers say that although it is not required, it is always a good idea to consult a lawyer about writing a will. This is because once you are dead you will not be available to explain what you intended when you wrote the document. This fact has led to the development of a lot of law about wills. Besides, courts take a very technical approach to interpreting wills; if you make a mistake, the court may invalidate your will altogether or may interpret something in a different way than you intended. A lawyer can draft your will using precise language that will make it clear what you intended and will make sure that all of the formalities required by the law are followed.

Many people put off writing a will. They think it will be expensive and not worthwhile if they do not have a lot of property or money. But the good news is that if you are over sixty and you do not have a large estate, you probably can have a will drafted for you for free or for a small fee (see the section entitled "Getting Help" later in this chapter). Even if you pay a lawyer to draft your will, it is a worthwhile investment. You can be assured that your property will be distributed as you intend.

WRITING YOUR OWN WILL

Can you write your own will and still feel confident that it will accomplish what you want? You can if you meet the following conditions:

- You do not have a large estate. Currently estates under $650,000 are not subject to federal estate taxes, but this limit is scheduled to increase to $1,000,000 over the next few years.
- You plan to leave your entire estate to your spouse or to divide it evenly among all of your children.
- Your will does not transfer property outside your immediate family, which would be subject to New Jersey taxes.

If you still want to write your own will, you can. If you write your will *in your own handwriting* and sign it yourself (this is called a holographic will), it should be valid in New Jersey. If you do this, make sure it is very clear that you intend the document to serve as your will by writing that it is your will. If you type your will, two witnesses who will not receive anything in the will must sign it, attesting that they have seen you signing your will. But if you write your own will you may not accomplish what you have set out to do. That is the situation Ethel has created.

If your estate is small and what you want to accomplish with a will is straightforward, you can complete your will on your own. Your only concern should be making sure that you meet the requirements for a valid will. By *straightforward* I mean that you are dividing property relatively equally among your family members, leaving all property to your spouse, or something similar. But there are many ways that you can alter this basic scheme; depending on your family's needs and what you own, some alternative might make sense. You do not want to complicate the situation or run the risk that what you want will not be done because your will does not meet the requirements of the law. So even if your assets are limited, there may be reason to consult an attorney. Doing so is not necessarily costly; you may be entitled to free or low-cost services to draft and execute your will.

If you have substantial assets or a nontraditional family, it is essential that you have a will. If your assets are substantial, an effective estate plan can ensure that your property will be handled as you wish and that no more estate taxes than necessary must be paid. If you wish to leave property to people outside of a traditional family, only a will can accomplish that for you. The law assumes that you are married and want your property to go to your spouse and children, and that is what will happen if you do not have a will. If you are not married and do not have children, the state will choose which relatives are to receive your estate or, if you have none, will keep your estate itself.

GETTING HELP. County Offices on Aging and some county Surrogate's Offices offer legal help, including the preparation of wills, at no cost or reduced cost depending on your circumstances. See appendixes A and D for information on locating these agencies.

LEGAL REQUIREMENTS FOR A VALID WILL

The person who is directing the distribution of his or her estate by signing a will is the testator. The law requires that a formal process be followed that entails a written will signed by the testator and witnessed by two people. If the testator is physically unable to sign the document, he or she can instruct someone else to sign for him or her. The person signing must sign the testator's name while in the presence and under the direction of the testator. The witnesses must both be present at the time of the signing. A will must be in writing. It is not enough to tell someone what you want done with your property. You can write down what you want and sign it. If the document is in your own handwriting and signed by you, it will be considered a valid will even without all the formalities of a will. But it must be written, and, as has been discussed, a formal will is still going to make things easier for your family and heirs than a handwritten will.

Anyone who is over eighteen years of age and competent may sign a will directing the disposition of his or her property after death. In order to be considered competent, a person must meet three requirements. First, the testator must have an understanding of what makes up his or her estate. If you think you own nothing but an old car and a cat when in fact you own a house and a dog and a collection of antique books, a court might find that you were not competent to make a will.

Second, the testator must recognize the "natural objects of one's bounty." If you have five surviving children and three grandchildren but you write your will as if you have only two children and neither of them is living, that can raise questions about your competence and hence about the validity of your will. With certain exceptions (discussed a bit later), you have a free hand to decide who will receive your property. But if you act as if you do not know who your natural heirs are, the law may decide that you were not competent to make a will. Third, you must have a plan for how your property is to be distributed. This simply means that you must define how the property should be divided or who should receive it all, which is the point of writing a will.

WHAT CANNOT BE DONE BY A WILL

A will gives you the opportunity to decide exactly how you want your property distributed after your death. If you do not have a will, the law of intestate succession controls who gets your property. Under this law the state decides who will receive your property by distributing it to your surviving family members using a fixed formula, with no accounting for different needs. A will, on the other hand, will allow you to distribute your property unevenly or to leave out some people who might expect to receive your property. But there are a few limits to what you can accomplish with a will. For instance, you cannot leave your spouse out of your will and deny him or her all of your property. If you do this, the law will allow your spouse to take a fixed percentage of your total estate regardless of what you provided in your will.

You can disinherit a child, but you should do it explicitly. If you simply do not mention one or more of your natural or adopted children, in some circumstances the law will assume that you made a mistake and fix this mistake by giving the omitted child the same percentage he or she would have received if you had not made a will. So if you have four children and you leave property to three of them, the omitted child could still receive a fourth of your property. If, on the other hand, you state in your will that you choose not to leave anything to one or more of your children, that choice will be respected. You are not required to leave property to your children (N.J.S.A. 3B:5–16).

There are two other ways you can leave a child out of your will that will be enforced by a court: you can leave all or substantially all of your estate to the other parent of the omitted child, or you can provide for the child by making a transfer of property outside of your will. If you do either of these things, the law will assume that you have made provision for the omitted child. But in either of these cases a lengthy and expensive court process may be necessary to enforce your wishes, so it is better to explicitly state in your will if you intend for one or more of your children not to receive property through your will. Otherwise, if you fail to provide for a child that child can challenge your will in order to receive a share of your estate equal to what he or she would have received if you had died intestate (without a will).

You cannot use a will to change beneficiaries of life insurance or to change the recipients of other nonprobate assets. As was mentioned earlier, nonprobate assets are things you own that have designated beneficiaries (such as life insurance) or that you own jointly with someone else. If you have a joint bank account with one of your three children and your will specifies that all of your money is to be divided equally among them, the joint holder of the bank account is entitled to all the money in the account on the day of your death. Your three children, including the one with whom you had a joint account, will equally divide the money in all your other bank accounts, but not the joint account. Any property you and another person hold jointly as "joint tenants with right of survivorship" will pass directly to the person who holds the property jointly with you. Your will cannot change this.

On the other hand, if you and another person hold property as "tenants in common," your share of the property will be distributed as you direct in your will; the other tenant will continue to own his or her share after your death. For instance, if you and your sister own a beach house together as tenants in common, you can pass your half to your children in your will. Your sister will continue to own half of the property until her death, when she can leave her share to whomever she chooses.

MAKING CHANGES TO YOUR WILL

There are two ways to make changes to your will. The first, and the one I recommend, is simply to execute a new will. This process invalidates the old will and makes your new wishes as to the distribution of your property very clear. The second way to change your will is to add a codicil, an addition to an existing will. But a codicil must be executed with all of the formality of a will, so it is just as complicated as executing a new will. It can also add confusion if it is not clear how the codicil affects the provisions of the original will. Codicils made much more sense before the age of computers. Now, with the advent of computerized word processing, it is much easier to revise your old will, create an entirely new will, and sign it in front of witnesses so it will be properly acknowledged.

One way you should not make changes in your will is by writing on the original will itself. It is not effective to cross out something in your will or add information in the margins. And doing this runs the risk that you will create confusion about what you wanted, which is the last thing you want to do.

WHAT TO DO WITH YOUR WILL ONCE IT IS COMPLETED

It is a good idea to keep a copy of your will with your important papers at home and to keep the original in your safe deposit box or in a safe deposit box maintained by your lawyer. By keeping a copy with your important papers, you will make it easier for your executor to locate your will when necessary. If the original is kept somewhere else, such as at the bank, put a note with the copy stating where the original is kept.

If you decide to change or update your will, follow the instructions in the preceding section. If you execute a new will, replace both the original and the copy so that it will still be clear what you want done. If you decide that you simply do not want your existing will any more, it is important that you destroy all copies so that no one can argue that you simply lost the original. If an original is lost or believed to be lost, it is possible for the probate court to admit a copy and follow the instructions in that document. If that is no longer what you want, you need to make that clear. Remember, you will not be around to tell the court what you meant to do.

PROVIDING FOR CHILDREN WITH DISABILITIES

Earlier in this chapter you read the story of Ethel, who wants to make special provisions for her daughter, Betty. Because Betty has a disability and cannot work, Ethel wants to make sure that Betty will be provided for and will be able to continue living in Ethel's house once Ethel is gone. But Betty also receives government benefits. If the benefits she receives are based on need, receiving an inheritance from Ethel may mean that the benefits will be withdrawn until Betty has spent all the money she inherits.

Ethel needs to write a will that will make special provisions for Betty. A "special needs trust" will allow her to provide for Betty without making her ineligible for government benefits. Ethel is under no obligation to provide for her other children in her will, but if she wants to leave some of her property to each of her three children, a will will allow her to make the division she wants and to provide for Betty as she sees fit.

UNDERSTANDING THE LAW

A special needs trust (also known as a supplemental needs trust) is a trust set up to provide resources for a person with a disability without making him or her ineligible for government benefits. Many government benefits are awarded based on need; a person who has assets, such as money from an inheritance, will be denied benefits until the inheritance has been spent. Using a trust is a legal way to allow the person with a disability to continue receiving benefits for basic living expenses and medical care and to use the inheritance to pay for other expenses that would not be paid for by the government benefits. It is important to pay attention to eligibility for benefits when considering how to leave assets to a person with a disability.

In the example, Ethel wants to help her daughter, Betty. But Ethel does not have enough money to provide for all of Betty's needs. Creating a trust puts responsibility as to how to spend the money in the trust in the hands of a trustee, who, in Ethel's case, can be anyone she chooses except Betty. Since Betty will not have control of the money, the government will not withdraw her benefits. A special needs trust will allow the trustee to provide for extras that Betty's benefits do not cover. So if Betty receives enough in government benefits to pay for food and housing, the trust might pay for books and extra clothing.

Assets that are held in a special needs trust can be used for the benefit of the person with a disability, but he or she cannot control the way in which they are used. If the assets were left directly to the individual or in a trust that the person with a disability controls, the government will consider them assets that should be spent for that person's support. If the trust is set up in accordance with the law, the person with a disability will not be able to decide when and how to spend the money independently, but at the same time the government will not count the property in awarding benefits.

A SAMPLE WILL

The following is the format for a basic will. It shows you the structure of a simple will, and in the notes are comments to help you understand the various provisions.

Last Will and Testament

of

[Your name][1]

I, [your name], residing in the town of [your town], County of [your county], and state of New Jersey, being of sound and disposing mind and memory, do hereby make, publish, and declare this to be my last will and testament, hereby revoking all wills and codicils heretofore made or executed by me.

First: I direct that all of my just debts, my funeral expenses, expenses of my last illness, and costs of administering my estate be paid as soon as practicable after my death.[2]

Second: I may include with this will a written statement disposing of certain items of tangible personal property not otherwise disposed of by this will. Said statement will be signed by me and may have the date of this will or a later date.[3]

Third: I hereby make the following specific bequests:[4]

I leave to my sister, [name], the sum of $500 if she survives me by sixty (60) days.[5]

---

1. The information in brackets should be personalized as appropriate.

2. This has to be done whether you include it in the will or not. But it serves as a clear instruction to your executor that this is to be done promptly.

3. By including this clause you give yourself the option to include a list of particular items that you would like certain individuals to receive. It will be much easier to change this list than to change the entire will, so it is useful to list smaller items about which you might change your mind. The possibility of writing such a list does not preclude your including specific bequests in the will itself. If you include such a clause in your will, follow through and write this list. You can always change it later, but if you never write a list some of your property may not go to the persons you intended.

4. These are some basic examples. Specific bequests can be listed for any identifiable items you want to leave to particular individuals. You can either choose an alternative if the named individual does not survive you, or allow the item to be distributed with your residual estate. Examples of both are given.

5. By requiring that a named individual survive you by a set number of days in order to inherit your property, you limit the confusion that might result

I leave to the Jones Foundation, of [address], whatever car, if any, I own at the time of my death.

I leave to my friend Mary Smith, currently residing at 42 Ocean Drive, Barnacle, New Jersey, my diamond earrings, if she survives me by sixty (60) days. If she does not survive me by 60 days, I leave my diamond earrings to my sister.

Fourth: I hereby leave my house and property, known as [complete address of house], to my three children, *per stirpes* and not *per capita*.[6]

Fifth: All the rest, residue, and remainder of my estate, whether real, personal, or mixed, wheresoever situated and of whatsoever the same may consist, including any lapsed legacies and any property over which I may have the power of appointment or other disposition that I have not otherwise validly exercised or released, and including any interest I have in real estate at [property address], I hereby give, devise, and bequeath unto [name of person to receive all property not otherwise disposed of in this will] if she survives me for a period of not less than sixty (60) days. In the event that [name of first recipient] shall predecease me or fails to survive me for a period of sixty (60) days, I give, devise, and bequeath all the rest, residue, and remainder of my estate, to [name of person to receive remainder of property if first recipient does not survive testator].[7]

---

if the two of you should die together or very close together in time. If you do not want the gift to go into the recipient's estate, this language requires that it be clear that he or she has survived you.

6. Although I try to make wills as straightforward and clear as possible, this bit of legal Latin is very important when you want to leave property to a group, such as your children. The question being addressed is this: if one of the group does not survive you, who should receive his or her share? If you have three children and one does not survive you, *per capita* means that the other two would share the gift (here, the house). *Per stirpes,* on the other hand, means that if one of your three children does not survive you but has children of his or her own, that child's share will go to his or her children.

7. This language, the residuary clause, is intended to be a catchall clause, allowing any property you do not specifically mention (and possibly do not even own at the time you sign your will) to be distributed in accordance with your wishes. This clause can be used to distribute all of your estate if there is one person or a limited group of people you wish to receive your property ("to all of my children living at the time of my death"), or it can simply cover any small

Sixth: I hereby name, constitute, and appoint [name] to be executor of this, my last will and testament. If for any reason [name of first choice] should fail to qualify or cease to be qualified, I hereby name, constitute, and appoint [name of second choice] as executor in her place. It is my wish that none of the executors herein named shall be required to give bond or other security in this or any other jurisdiction.

Seventh: I grant without limitation unto my executor, including any substitute or successor, all powers given to executors by the laws of the state of New Jersey at the time of my execution of this last will and testament, and all further powers that may later be enacted into the said laws.

In witness whereof, I have hereunto set my hand and seal to this, my last will and testament, this [date] day of [month], [year].

_____[Your signature]_____

Signed, sealed, published, and declared by [your name] on the day and year aforesaid as and for [his or her] last will and testament, in our presence, at [his or her] request, in the presence of each other, all being present at the same time and the testator signing first, we have hereunto subscribed our names as witnesses.

_____[Signature of witness]_____
_____[Printed name of witness] of_____
_____[Witness's address]_____
_____[Signature of witness]_____
_____[Printed name of witness] of_____
_____[Witness's address]_____

_____

items you did not think to include among more specific bequests. It is very important that you make some provision for the residuary so that nothing unexpected will not be covered by your will.

Acknowledgment and Affidavit
Relating to Execution of Will[8]

I, [your name], the testator, sign my name to this instrument this [date] day of [month], [year], and being duly sworn, do hereby declare to the undersigned authority that I sign and execute this instrument as my last will and testament and that I sign it willingly, that I execute it as my free and voluntary act for the purposes expressed therein, and that I am 18 years of age or older, of sound mind, and under no constraint or undue influence.

___[Your signature]___

We, [name of witness] and [name of witness], the witnesses, sign our names to this instrument, and, being duly sworn, do hereby declare to the undersigned authority that the testator signs and executes this instrument as [his or her] last will, and that [he or she] signs it willingly and that each of us, in the presence and hearing of the testator, hereby signs this will as witness to the testator's signing, and that to the best of our knowledge the testator is 18 years of age or older, of sound mind, and under no constraint or undue influence.

___[Signature of witness]___

___[Signature of witness]___

State of New Jersey
County of ___[name of county]___

Subscribed, sworn to, and acknowledged before me by [your name], the testator, and subscribed and sworn to before me by [name of witness] and [name of witness], witnesses, this [date] day of [month], [year].

___[Signature and seal of notary public]___

---

8. This affidavit is a separate document that should be included with your will. It establishes the circumstances of your signing the will and allows the court to admit the will to probate without the witnesses' appearing in court. It essentially stands as the testimony of the witnesses with regard to what they observed and did. It must be signed in the presence of a notary public or an attorney.

The government will have to decide whether the money placed in trust is available for the support of the person with a disability. If it is, the government will think it should be used instead of relying on government benefits. If, however, it is specified that the assets are to be used only to supplement the needs of the person with a disability and the person with a disability cannot decide to use it in any other way, the government will provide benefits to cover the need for support (assuming the person with a disability is otherwise eligible). Since the government will look carefully at a special needs trust to determine if it affects eligibility, it is important to consult an attorney to be sure the trust is established correctly.

7. Powers of Attorney and Alternative Financial Arrangements

As Joe has gotten older he has relied more and more on his daughter to help him with tasks such as paying bills. She writes checks and he signs them, but she is concerned that the day will come when he will no longer be physically able to sign the checks. Joe's daughter has asked him to sign a general power of attorney so that she can take care of his financial affairs if it becomes necessary. Joe is not sure that he wants to give his daughter too much power, as he is afraid that she will place him in a nursing home against his wishes.

Joe should make arrangements to ensure that his financial affairs will be taken care of if he is no longer able to manage them himself, but a general power of attorney is only one possible solution. Joe is right to be concerned that a general power of attorney might allow his daughter to take actions he would not approve of, since it would give her the power to do anything that he would otherwise be able to do for himself. Instead of giving his daughter such broad power, he could make her a cosigner on his checking account or give her a power of attorney limited to banking or one that would be in effect only if he were to become disabled (although the latter option poses certain problems that will be discussed a bit later). All these options are discussed in this chapter.

POWERS OF ATTORNEY

A power of attorney is a document that authorizes an agent, referred to as the "attorney in fact," to act for the signer of the document, referred to as the principal. If Joe in the story signs a power of attorney, he is the principal. If he wants his daughter to act for him, she will become his attorney in fact. Creating a power of attorney is not difficult. Such a document is written to show a third party, such as a bank, that the attorney in fact has the power to act for the principal. A power of attorney lasts until it is revoked or until the principal dies. It is not possible to use a power of attorney after the death of the person who created it.

You do not give up the power to act for yourself when you give someone a power of attorney. You are creating an agent who can act for you. But you are still the principal. You can still take action for yourself, including revoking the power of attorney if you no longer want the agent to act for you.

Note that although a power of attorney names someone your "attorney in fact," the person you appoint does *not* have to be a lawyer. You are simply naming someone to act for you, and it should be someone you trust. It is important to be sure you that you trust the person you are naming as your agent and that you understand what power you are giving your agent. There are different types of powers of attorney, which will be discussed a bit later. The form that is included at the end of this chapter is for what is called a general durable power of attorney, and it should be sufficient to allow your agent to act for you in most situations. It is not very specific, so it might be useful to create a more detailed power of attorney if your agent is likely to deal with more complex financial or real estate transactions. Please note that a general power of attorney is not sufficient to avoid a guardianship if you have substantial assets; you will want an attorney to prepare a detailed power of attorney for you.

GENERAL AND LIMITED POWERS OF ATTORNEY. Powers of attorney can be either general or limited. This means that either you give your agent the power to do anything you could do for yourself (general) or you give your agent the power to conduct a specific transaction, such as authorizing someone to sign documents for you at a real estate closing (limited). A power of attorney that is limited to banking might be sufficient to meet the needs of Joe in the story at the beginning of this chapter.

It is important to realize that a general power of attorney gives your agent a great deal of power, since it will allow your appointed attorney in fact to make decisions about your money and your property. The agent is supposed to act in your interest and to do what you instruct, but he or she could withdraw money from your bank account without your approval and use it for his or her own purposes. In such a case you would have to try to get the money back from the agent; you could not fault the bank for giving your agent the money. The power of attorney document tells the bank that giving money to your agent is the same as giving it to you, and the bank is right to follow this instruction. If your agent withdraws money against your will, the bank has done nothing wrong.

DURABLE POWERS OF ATTORNEY. When using a power of attorney for planning purposes, as Joe wants to do, you should specify that the power being given is "durable." This means that the power of attorney will continue to be effective if you become incapacitated and are no longer able to take care of your own affairs. It is necessary to specify in the document that the power of attorney is durable and will survive your incapacity, because if you do not state this explicitly the law will assume that you want the power of attorney to last only as long as you are capable.

Historically, powers of attorney were intended to allow someone to do what you would otherwise do for yourself, so if you were no longer able to act, neither was your attorney in fact. In contrast, a durable power of attorney will allow someone to act for you even when you no longer can act, and therefore makes it less likely that the appointment of a guardian will be necessary when you cannot act for yourself (see chapter 9).

SPRINGING DURABLE POWERS OF ATTORNEY. So far we have discussed creating a general durable power of attorney, and that is the type of document that appears at the end of this chapter. There is one further consideration, and that is whether to make this document a "springing" durable power of attorney. A springing durable power of attorney does not give power to the attorney in fact at the time you sign the document; it gives him or her power only at such time as you become incapacitated. Creating such a power of attorney is often an appealing idea, since it does not transfer power to the agent until it is really necessary. But there are some big drawbacks to this approach.

Using a power of attorney requires establishing to the satisfaction of a third party that the attorney in fact has the authority necessary to act for you. This generally requires establishing that the document is authentic, that it is recent enough to still be believable, and that the person named in the document is the person attempting to act. But if the document states that the agent does not have any power to act until the principal becomes incapacitated, the third party will also have to know whether that contingency has occurred. Since this will probably involve showing that doctors have decided you are no longer able to make decisions for yourself, you can imagine that it will not be simple to show to the satisfaction of a financial or other institution that this is the case.

WHAT TO DO WITH A COMPLETED POWER OF ATTORNEY. You can decide whether you want to give the completed document to your agent at the time you sign it or to keep it with your other important papers and tell the agent where to find it when it is necessary to use it. By giving it to your agent when you create the document, you will make it easier to use. If you want your agent to be able to use the power of attorney only when you become incapacitated, you can keep the document itself so that it cannot be used now. But if you do this be sure the agent knows where it is and will be able to get access to the original when it is needed. The agent will need to have the original to show to a bank or other institution.

TERMINATING A POWER OF ATTORNEY. If you no longer want your agent to act for you, revoke the power of attorney in writing, and let affected parties (your agent and your financial institutions) know that the previous power of attorney is no longer in effect. To the extent possible, get back and destroy all copies of the old power of attorney so that there will be no question about whether they are still in effect. This will protect you if your attorney in fact attempts to continue using the power of attorney after you revoke it.

FINANCIAL CONSIDERATIONS. Note that even if you sign a general durable power of attorney, it is still advisable to go to your bank and ask for the bank's power of attorney form and complete that as well. Some banks and other institutions are very nervous about using powers of attorney, because they are concerned that if they follow an invalid power of attorney you will sue them for handling your money or property improperly. This can lead them to make it difficult to use powers of attorney in some circumstances. Banks prefer to rely on their own forms, and by signing your bank's form you will make it easier for your attorney in fact to act for you at the bank. But note that although some banks might object to using a power of attorney that is not on their own form or that was not recently executed, there is no legal basis for this objection. Just be sure the document you sign specifically gives your agent the power to conduct banking transactions (as does the sample form on pages 82–83).

It is easy to sign a power of attorney just for banking. Just ask your bank for their form, and complete it according to their instructions. This power of attorney will be effective only at the bank at which you sign it, so if you have accounts at several banks you will

---

QUESTIONS TO ASK YOURSELF ABOUT YOUR POWER OF ATTORNEY

■ Do you trust the person you are appointing to always act in your best interest?

■ Are you giving your agent sufficient power to do whatever might need to be done, such as doing your banking, selling real estate, and so on?

■ Does your agent have the original power of attorney document or know where to find it?

---

need to do this at each bank where you want to give your agent the power to act for you. But if there is someone available whom you would trust with broader powers, it is advisable to create a general power of attorney in addition in order to take care of business you might not anticipate.

A power of attorney can be very important if you become incapable of managing your own affairs, and it may allow you to avoid guardianship proceedings. But if you have substantial assets you will want to complete a more detailed power of attorney form than the one provided on pages 82–83. A general power of attorney is not enough to allow your attorney in fact to make gifts, for example. If it becomes necessary for your agent to make transfers of your funds to prepare you for Medicaid eligibility, he or she will have to seek a guardianship unless you have created a power of attorney with gift-making authority and other types of detailed authority. You should ask an attorney to prepare a power of attorney that will address both Medicaid and tax considerations.

ALTERNATIVES TO POWERS OF ATTORNEY

There are some alternatives to signing a general durable power of attorney that you should consider. If, like Joe, you are not sure that you can comfortably give broad power to one person, you should consider whether you can use some or all of the following strategies to take care of your affairs.

A SAMPLE DURABLE POWER OF ATTORNEY

The following is the format for a basic durable power of attorney. It shows you the structure of such a document, and in the notes are comments to help you understand the various provisions. Note that this form will not give your agent the power to engage in estate planning or make transfers for Medicaid eligibility if you become incompetent. If your assets are substantial, use a more detailed power of attorney.

Durable Power of Attorney

I, [your name][1], of [street address and town], New Jersey, hereby appoint [name of person to be appointed attorney in fact] of [street address and town], New Jersey, as my attorney in fact, to act for me and in my name and for my use and benefit. By signing this document, I intend to create a durable power of attorney. This durable power of attorney shall not be affected by my subsequent disability or incapacity and shall remain effective until my death or until revoked by me in writing.[2]

I grant my attorney in fact full power and authority over all my property, real and personal, and authorize [him or her] to do and perform all and every act that I, as owner of the property, could do or perform, and I hereby ratify and confirm all that my attorney in fact shall do or cause to be done under this durable power of attorney.[3] In particular, I authorize my attorney in fact to conduct banking transactions as set forth in section 2 of P.L. 1991, Chapter 95 (N.J.S.A. 46:2B-11).[4]

The powers conferred on my attorney in fact by this durable power of attorney may be exercised by my attorney in fact alone,

---

1. The information in brackets should be personalized as appropriate.

2. This language makes this a durable power of attorney so that the power continues even if the principal is no longer able to act for himself or herself. It will end with the death of the principal unless previously revoked.

3. This sentence makes this a general power of attorney. It allows the agent to do everything the principal could do and states that any actions taken by the agent are approved by the principal.

4. By stating that the agent is authorized to conduct banking transactions, the principal is taking advantage of using a single document to give the agent general powers. Without this specific provision, a bank may refuse to accept a general power of attorney.

and my attorney in fact's signature may be accepted by any third person or organization as fully authorized by me and with the same force and effect as if I were personally present, competent, and acting on my own behalf.[5]

No person or organization that relies on this durable power of attorney or any representation my attorney in fact makes regarding [his or her] authority, including but not limited to: (i) the fact that this durable power of attorney has not been revoked; (ii) the fact that I, [your name], was competent to execute this power of attorney; and (iii) the authority of my attorney in fact under this durable power of attorney shall incur any liability to me or my estate, heirs, successors, or assigns because of such reliance on this durable power of attorney or on any such representation by my attorney in fact.[6]

Executed this [date] day of [month], [year].

<u>   [Your signature]   </u>

Witnesses

<u>   [Signature of witness]   </u>

<u> [Witness's printed name and address] </u>

<u>   [Signature of witness]   </u>

<u> [Witness's printed name and address] </u>

Notarization
State of New Jersey
County of [name of county]

Subscribed, sworn to, and acknowledged before me by [your name] this [date] day of [month, year].

<u> [Signature and seal of notary public] </u>

---

5. This makes it clear that the signature or presence of the principal is not necessary.

6. This paragraph assures any party that accepts this document that there is no liability for doing so. It is intended to make it easier to use this power of attorney, because the party accepting it does not have to make its own decision about whether the document has been revoked, the principal was competent at the time it was signed, or the agent has the general authority granted under the document.

First, you should consider a limited power of attorney, which has already been discussed. It is easy to give a friend or family member the power to act for you in a more limited way by signing a limited power of attorney, particularly for banking.

You can also use joint ownership to give someone a means to act for you. If you add someone else's name to your bank account, that person will become a joint owner of the account and can then write checks or withdraw funds just as you would. But note that this will also allow the person to write checks for himself or herself; the person will own the account equally with you, so even if you deposit all the money in the account the other person will have the same right you do to take the money out. If you want to limit the possibility of this happening, consider separating accounts and putting in the joint account only enough money to cover expenses. This will allow you to limit how much money the joint owner can access.

Trusts are another means to give someone else the power to act with regard to your money or property. Because of the complexities of trust law, it is necessary to see an attorney to prepare a trust. A trust becomes a legal entity that must pay taxes, and the property held in trust is controlled by one or more trustees. By putting property in trust and naming someone a trustee, you will give the trustee the ability to act with regard to only the property held in the trust. This will allow you to choose who has control and the property over which they can exercise this control.

Finally, it is possible to assign someone to receive benefit checks on your behalf. Your Social Security check can go directly to a "representative payee" rather than to you. The representative payee will then be bound to spend the money on your behalf. If you need someone to spend just the benefits you receive and you are willing to have the money go directly to the person you designate, this strategy can allow you to avoid giving anyone power over your bank accounts. But using a representative payee will not provide many protections, since the Social Security Administration will not keep an eye on what a representative payee does with your money. If you do not trust someone enough to give him or her any other authority, it is probably not wise to trust this person with your benefits check.

A note of caution is warranted here. It is possible for someone to become your representative payee without your permission. If someone represents to the Social Security Administration that you are incapable of managing your affairs, the administration may allow that person to become a payee without the formalities of a guardianship proceeding. If this happens, immediately contact the Social Security Administration. If you need additional assistance, contact a lawyer (see appendix B) or Adult Protective Services (see appendix E).

8. Advance Directives

Martha cared for her brother after he was incapacitated by a stroke, and she visited him regularly after he moved into a nursing home. Now that he is gone, she is afraid that someday she will be similarly incapacitated, and she feels strongly that she does not want to have to go through what she saw her brother experience before his death. She wonders if there is some way to tell her doctor not to keep her alive if there is no hope that she will recover.

What Martha can do is to sign an advance directive for health care. Such a document will do two things: it will allow Martha to put into writing her wish to refuse medical treatment if there is no hope that she will recover, and it will allow her to name the person she would like to make health care decisions for her if she is unable to make them for herself. It is helpful for her to give both types of instructions, because they serve different purposes, but she can decide she wants to do only one and not the other.

WHEN PATIENTS CANNOT SPEAK FOR THEMSELVES

The problem Martha faces is one that concerns many people. Doctors now have the ability to keep people alive long after they are no longer able to speak for themselves or after they have any hope of recovering. The legal problem is how to determine whether the patient wishes to refuse medical treatment when the patient is unable to speak for himself or herself. If the patient is conscious and able to say what he or she wants, that patient has the right to decide the medical treatment he or she will receive, including the right to refuse life-sustaining treatment. But what happens if the patient is comatose or otherwise incapable of communicating his or her wishes? If the patient has planned ahead and stated these wishes in advance, the doctors and medical staff can be guided by the patient's own instructions. If the patient has not left such instructions, someone else will have to make the decisions. Family members can make some decisions, but it is difficult to refuse treatment without instructions from the patient.

By signing an advance directive for health care Martha can state her wishes, and she can also choose who will make health care decisions

WHEN DO ADVANCE DIRECTIVES TAKE EFFECT?

Advance directives take effect only when you are no longer able to express your wishes. As long as you are still able to state your wishes, the instructions in these documents do not go into effect.

for her if her instructions do not cover the type of problem that arises. The document Martha signs will tell the doctors and the hospital what to do. But if there are problems that the document does not address, by appointing someone she trusts as a health care proxy to make health care decisions for her Martha can be confident that these important decisions will be made by someone who understands her wishes.

Although Martha in our story would choose not to be given life-sustaining treatment if she had little or no chance of recovery, you can use the same documents to state your desire to receive all treatment available. It is entirely up to you to decide what circumstances you would like to address in the document and what decisions you want to make in advance. Read the document carefully before you sign, and make sure you understand what it is that you are deciding. It is also important that you choose a health care proxy who understands your wishes and whom you trust to follow your instructions.

The document that states the decisions Martha would make for herself is called an instruction directive, but it is generally known as a living will. The document that appoints someone else to make health care decisions for Martha if she is unable to make such decisions for herself is called a proxy directive. If Martha wants to do both things at the same time, she can complete one form, called a combined advance directive for health care, which is both an instruction directive and a proxy directive in one form. The form at the end of this chapter is a combined advance directive.

A SAMPLE COMBINED ADVANCE DIRECTIVE

The following is a sample format for a combined advance directive. This sample form allows you to both express your wishes as to your health care and appoint a proxy to advocate for you and to make any decisions not covered by your statement of your wishes. This combined advance directive was developed by the New Jersey Bioethics Commission and is reprinted here with permission.

Combined Advance Directive for Health Care

I understand that as a competent adult I have the right to make decisions about my health care. There may come a time when I am unable, due to physical or mental incapacity, to make my own health care decisions. In these circumstances, those caring for me will need direction concerning my care and they will require information about my values and health care wishes in order to provide the guidance and authority needed to make decisions on my behalf.

I, [your name], hereby declare and make known to my family, physician, and others my instructions and wishes for my future health care. I direct that all health care decisions, including decisions to accept or refuse any treatment, service, or procedure used to diagnose, treat, or care for my physical or mental condition and decisions to provide, withhold, or withdraw life-sustaining measures, be made in accordance with my wishes as expressed in this document. This instruction directive shall take effect in the event I become unable to make my own health care decisions, as determined by the physician who has primary responsibility for my care and any necessary confirming determinations. I direct that this document become part of my permanent medical records.

Part One: Designation of a Health Care Representative

I hereby designate my [daughter/son/friend][1], [name], who currently resides at [address], as my health care representative to make any and all health care decisions for me, including decisions

---

1. The information in brackets should be personalized as appropriate. Here you identify your relationship to the person you are appointing as your health care proxy.

to accept or refuse any treatment, service, or procedure used to diagnose or treat my physical or mental condition and decisions to provide, withhold, or withdraw life-sustaining measures. I direct my representative to make decisions on my behalf in accordance with my wishes as stated in this document or as otherwise known to him or her. In the event my wishes are not clear or a situation arises I did not anticipate, my health care representative is authorized to make decisions in my best interest based upon what is known of my wishes.[2]

I have discussed the terms of this designation with my health care representative, and he or she has willingly agreed to accept the responsibility for acting on my behalf.[3]

If the person I have designated above is unable, unwilling, or unavailable to act as my health care representative, I hereby designate to act as my health care representative [name], who currently resides at [address].[4]

Part Two: Statement of My Wishes Concerning
My Future Health Care

To inform those responsible for my care of my specific wishes, I make the following statement of my personal views regarding my health care (choose and initial either):

1. ____ I direct that all medically appropriate measures be provided to sustain my life, regardless of my physical or mental condition.

2. ____ There are circumstances in which I would not want my life to be prolonged by further medical treatment. In these circumstances life-sustaining measures should not be initiated, and if they have been they should be discontinued. In the follow-

---

2. You are giving the proxy the power to make any necessary health care decisions only when you can no longer make them for yourself. You are also instructing the proxy to follow the letter and the spirit of your instructions.

3. It is important that the person you appoint know and agree to this designation. The appointment will work only if the proxy acts in your interest.

4. By appointing an alternate you make it more likely that one of those you name will be available at the time he or she is needed. You could also appoint two proxies jointly, but that would require that they agree before acting, so be sure they will be able to work together.

ing I specify the circumstances in which I would choose to forego life-sustaining measures.[5]

a. ___ I realize that there may come a time when I am diagnosed as having an incurable and irreversible illness, disease, or condition. If this occurs and my attending physician and at least one additional physician who has personally examined me determine that my condition is terminal, I direct that life-sustaining measures which would serve only to artificially prolong my dying be withheld or discontinued. I also direct that I be given all medically appropriate care necessary to make me comfortable and to relieve my pain.

To me, *terminal condition* means that my physicians have determined that _____ .[6]

b. ___ If there should come a time when I become permanently unconscious and it is determined by my attending physician and at least one additional physician with appropriate expertise who has personally examined me that I have totally and irreversibly lost consciousness and my capacity for interaction with other people and my surroundings, I direct that life-sustaining measures be withheld or discontinued. I understand that I will not experience pain or discomfort in this condition, and I direct that I be given all medically appropriate care necessary to provide for my personal hygiene and dignity.[7]

c. ___ I realize that there may come a time when I am diagnosed as having an incurable and irreversible illness, disease, or condition that may not be terminal. My condition may cause me to experience severe and progressive physical or mental deterioration and/or permanent loss of capacities and faculties I

---

5. Choose the appropriate language to indicate whether you choose to have treatment terminated. If you choose to have treatment terminated, put your initials in the space at the beginning of each paragraph in the following section that you want to apply to you.

6. You can decide how close to death you must be before this option will come into effect. You could write, "I will die within a few days," "I will die within one week," "I will die within one month," "I will die within less than one year," or something similar.

7. This paragraph calls for the withdrawal of treatment if you are found to be permanently unconscious. Initial this paragraph only if you want treatment terminated under these circumstances.

value highly. If in the course of my medical care the burdens of continued life with treatment become greater than the benefits I experience, I direct that life-sustaining measures be withheld or discontinued. I also direct that I be given all medically appropriate care necessary to make me comfortable and to relieve pain.[8]

Examples of conditions that I find unacceptable are:[9]

_____

_____

_____

SPECIFIC INSTRUCTIONS REGARDING ARTIFICIALLY PROVIDED FLUIDS AND NUTRITION AND ABOUT CARDIOPULMONARY RESUSCITATION

1. ___ In the circumstances I initialed earlier, I also direct that artificially provided fluids and nutrition, such as by feeding tube or intravenous infusion, [be withheld or withdrawn and that I be allowed to die/be provided to the extent medically appropriate].[10]

2. ___ In the circumstances I initialed earlier, if I should suffer a cardiac arrest I also direct that cardiopulmonary resuscitation [not be provided and that I be allowed to die/be provided to preserve my life unless medically inappropriate or futile].[11]

3. ___ If neither of the above statements adequately expresses your wishes concerning artificially provided fluids and nutrition or CPR, please explain your wishes below.

_____

_____

_____

_____

8. This is the most expansive paragraph, providing for the withdrawal of treatment any time you have an incurable or irreversible condition that severely limits your enjoyment of life.

9. If you wish, you may specify in more detail the conditions in which you would choose to forego life-sustaining measures. You might include a description of faculties or capacities that, if irretrievably lost, would lead you to accept death rather than continue living.

10. Choose the phrase that describes your wishes.

11. The alternatives here allow you to indicate whether you want the intervention of CPR, which can restart your heart if it has stopped.

ADDITIONAL INSTRUCTIONS

Include any additional information about your health care preferences that is important to you and may help those concerned with your care to implement your wishes.

_____

_____

_____

BRAIN DEATH

Initial this statement only if it applies to you.

_____ To declare my death on the basis of the whole brain death standard would violate my personal religious beliefs. I therefore wish my death to be declared solely on the basis of the traditional criteria of irreversible cessation of cardiopulmonary (heartbeat and breathing) function.

I wish/do not wish to make an anatomical gift upon my death.[12]

_____

_____

_____

Signature and Witnesses

The original or a copy of this document has been given to the following people:[13]

_____ [Name]

_____ [Address]

_____ [Phone]

By writing this advance directive I inform those who may become entrusted with my health care of my wishes and intend to ease the burdens of decision making that this responsibility may impose. I have discussed the terms of this designation with my health care representative, and he or she has willingly agreed to accept the responsibility for acting on my behalf in accordance with this

---

12. If you wish to make anatomical gifts, indicate what you wish to include (specific organs, any organs that can be used, or your whole body).

13. Give the name, address, and phone number of each person to whom you have given a copy of the document. It is important to give a copy to your health care representative.

directive. I understand the purpose and effect of this document and sign it knowingly, voluntarily, and after careful deliberation.

_____[Signature]_____

_____[Date]_____

_____[Printed Name]_____

_____[Address]_____

Witnesses

I declare that the person who signed this document or asked another to sign this document on his or her behalf did so in my presence, that he or she is personally known to me, and that he or she appears to be of sound mind and free of duress or undue influence. I am 18 years of age or older, and am not designated by this or any other document as the person's health care representative or as an alternate health care representative.

_____[Signature]_____

_____[Date]_____

_____[Printed name]_____

_____[Address]_____

_____[Signature]_____

_____[Date]_____

_____[Printed name]_____

_____[Address]_____

GETTING HELP

There is a legally valid form for each of these directives, and it is available from the New Jersey Bioethics Commission, CN-061, Trenton, NJ 08625. The New Jersey Bioethics Commission has prepared a booklet with these forms and explanatory material. The booklet gives a list of the choices available for each part of the documents, and you can complete them yourself. Be sure to sign in front of witnesses.

If you go to a hospital, you have the right to have these forms included in your medical records. If there is an emergency, make sure someone (usually your proxy) has a copy to take to the hospital. Sometimes you will be told to complete these documents prior to admission to a health care facility, such as a nursing home. And sometimes the documents you are asked to sign will give instructions to terminate treatment if it becomes clear that you cannot recover. However, you cannot be forced to sign these documents if you do not want to. You also can complete the forms with instructions that everything possible be done for you. Do not feel compelled to agree to terminate treatment if that is not what you want.

UNDERSTANDING THE LAW

Mary has worked for years as a home health aide. She has seen many of the people she has cared for go to the hospital with living wills already signed, but still receive care beyond their instructions. She feels that living wills are not effective, so she does not want to sign one. She trusts her family to make the decisions she would have made for herself.

Unfortunately, Mary is correct in thinking that even a person with a living will sometimes receives unwanted care. Doctors do not always feel that the circumstances are consistent with a person's instructions. However, by signing a living will you make your wishes clear. If you do not put your instructions in writing, it will be even more difficult for your family and your doctor to know and carry out your instructions. Doctors and hospitals are much more likely to assume you want all treatment available if you have never put a different desire in writing. So although they are imperfect, living wills are the best approach available.

It is also very helpful to appoint a health care proxy so that it will be clear who you want to make health care decisions for you. If your family is available, your doctor will listen to their instructions, but by appointing one individual as your proxy, you will make it clearer who is to enforce your instructions. This is particularly important if you do not have immediate family available or if you do not trust your family to make the decisions you would make. Your health care proxy has the legal authority to make decisions for you, even if your family disagrees. This person can serve as your advocate and has the authority to change doctors for you if that is necessary in order to enforce your instructions.

9. Guardianship and Conservatorship

If you are unable to care for yourself and are mentally incompetent, a court can appoint a guardian to manage your affairs and make decisions for you. In order to appoint a guardian someone must file a petition with the superior court, and the court must decide that you are mentally incompetent. The court will then appoint a guardian to provide the assistance you need. Much like a guardian appointed for a minor child to provide for his or her care, a guardian for an incompetent adult is responsible for protecting and providing care and has the power to make decisions and spend money on behalf of the protected person.

If you live with your spouse at the time of the guardianship petition, the law requires that your spouse be named the guardian unless your spouse refuses or it is proven to the court that he or she is not able to serve or is unlikely to act in your best interest. Usually the court will appoint a family member or someone close to you as your guardian, but if no one is available to serve and you are over sixty, the New Jersey Public Guardian can be appointed to provide guardianship services.

Once a guardian is appointed, the guardian is responsible for making decisions for you, as well as managing your money and spending it for your benefit. It is possible for the court to appoint a "guardian of the person" and a separate "guardian of the estate." This action separates the functions of providing for your care and managing your finances, and when these functions are separate the two guardians must work together to make decisions for you. The guardian will be responsible to the court and must make reports to the court to assure it that everything is being done properly. The guardian receives 6 percent of your income and a small percentage of your assets each year.

If you are found incompetent and a guardian is appointed, but you subsequently return to competency, it will be necessary for you to go back to court to be judged competent. The judge will consider the circumstances, and if you are found to be competent the guardianship will be ended. The law provides that if you were incompetent because of alcoholism or drug abuse you must show that you have stopped drinking or using drugs for one year before a guardianship will be ended.

The imposition of a guardianship is an extreme measure. Once a person is found to be incompetent and in need of a guardian, he or she loses the ability to make decisions. This includes deciding where to live, whether to make a will, and who will be his or her doctor. The person under a guardianship also loses the right to marry. Guardianship is intended to provide necessary care for someone who is no longer able to make decisions.

There are circumstances in which you might need some assistance, but not to the extent that a guardianship implies. A conservatorship can be appropriate in this case. A conservatorship is provided to allow for more limited intervention than is provided by a guardianship. A conservator is appointed to provide financial services. The conservator may be an individual or a financial institution. If you have a conservator you can no longer make your own financial decisions. However, a conservatorship is a voluntary arrangement, so if you object the court will not impose a conservator on you.

UNDERSTANDING THE LAW

What are the differences between powers of attorney and guardianships? If you have appointed someone as your power of attorney, that person can act for you with whatever powers you have given him or her in the document (see chapter 7). This can delay or avoid the need for someone to be appointed as your guardian, because your bills will be paid and your affairs will be taken care of by the person you choose. The difference between a guardian and someone using a power of attorney is that you do not give up the ability to act for yourself when you give someone a power of attorney. The person you appoint has power parallel to yours; you can continue to act on your own behalf. You do not give up the ability to act—for instance, to write checks on your bank account, or to decide where to live. When a guardian has been appointed you lose the ability to act for yourself. A power of attorney that gives your agent specific powers can be a very powerful tool to avoid the need for a guardianship. If this is your goal, make sure your agent will have the specific power necessary to act for you. Consult an attorney if you want to develop a power of attorney with sufficient power to be certain to avoid a guardianship.

Although having a power of attorney can delay or eliminate the need for a guardian, it does not necessarily mean that a guardian will never be appointed. If a guardianship is created, the guardian will have the power to revoke a power of attorney, just as you have that power as long as you are capable of acting for yourself.

IV. FAMILY CONCERNS

This section includes information on divorce and remarriage, grand-parent visitation and custody, and abuse of the elderly. The previous section, "Personal Decision Making," was all about planning. If you make those decisions, sign the recommended documents, and thereby provide instructions about your wishes, you can avoid some problems and head off certain family conflicts. Although that is always the goal, there are times when conflicts arise no matter what your intentions. This section addresses these issues. Intergenerational conflicts can lead to grandparent visitation and custody concerns or even to elder abuse, and marital conflicts can lead to divorce. If you or someone you care about is facing these difficulties, the following chapters provide guidance on your rights and what steps you can take to address the problem.

Each chapter in this section gives you information to help you understand the relevant laws and what steps you can take to address the problems. Some typical questions that are answered are:

- My son is getting a divorce, and his wife will have custody of the children. How can I be sure I will still get to see my grandchildren?
- If my daughter cannot take care of her children, can I ask the court to place them with me?
- If I get a divorce, will I get alimony?
- I always stayed home and my spouse supported me. If we get a divorce, will I still get Social Security benefits?
- How can I afford a divorce lawyer if I do not have any money of my own?
- Can I stay in our home once we are divorced?
- When I said I wanted a divorce, my spouse hit me. Can I make him move out of our home? Can I get protection from the police?
- If I plan to marry again, can I make sure my children will inherit my property?
- I think the person who cares for me is taking money from my Social Security check. Is there anything I can do?
- My sister will not let me see our mother, who lives with her, and I am afraid she is not taking proper care of her. Can I make her let me visit?

10. Grandparent Visitation and Custody

As a grandparent, you want to establish and maintain a relationship with your grandchildren. This usually does not require any legal intervention, but sometimes family relationships do not go smoothly. In order to support the interest of children's knowing their grandparents, the law provides a remedy when families do not work such relationships out on their own.

VISITATION

Do you have a right to see your grandchildren? In New Jersey the answer is yes. Can you force them to visit you, even if their parents do not encourage it? Again, the answer is yes. But do you want to force them to visit you? That is a more difficult question to answer.

The New Jersey legislature passed a statute that gives courts the ability to order visitation between grandparents and their grandchildren, just as it might order visitation in a divorce action so that the noncustodial parent can see his or her children. The grandparent visitation statute is intended to allow grandparents to maintain a relationship with their grandchildren even when the parent to whom the grandparents are related dies or is divorced and the grandchildren live with the other parent. Even when a new spouse adopts the child, grandparents of a divorced parent have the right to request visitation to maintain a continued relationship. Furthermore, the statute allows grandparents to go to court to request visitation when the family is intact but for some reason the parents refuse to allow visits between grandparents and grandchildren.

For example, if Georgia fights with her daughter and they are no longer speaking, it is conceivable that Georgia could go to court and get an order to allow her to visit with her grandchildren even over her daughter's objections. Whether Georgia wants to do this—or whether the court will in fact order the visitation she is seeking—is another question, but the right to go to court to make such a request is clearly laid out in the statute (N.J.S.A. 9:2-7.1 et seq.).

UNDERSTANDING THE LAW. New Jersey's statute allows the grandparent of a child who lives in New Jersey to apply to the court for an order for visitation. If you apply for such an order, it is up to you to persuade the court that it is in the best interest of your grandchild to visit with you. This means that the burden is on you to persuade the judge that visitation is a good idea. It is not enough for you to want to visit; it must be good for your grandchild.

In order to decide whether an order will be issued, the court will consider a long list of factors, including the relationship you have with your grandchild; how long it has been since you have seen your grandchild; your relationship with the child's parents; whether granting your order will have a negative effect on your grandchild's relationship with the parent with whom he or she lives; any history you have of physical, emotional, or sexual abuse or neglect; and any other factor the judge thinks is relevant to deciding what is in the child's best interest.

As you look at this list of factors the judge will consider, think about not just what you would tell the judge about why you should be granted a visitation order, but what the parents will say if they do not want you to visit your grandchild. If there have ever been allegations of abuse against you, for example, it is unlikely the judge will decide to award you visitation. If you have not had a lot of contact with your grandchildren, it will be difficult to persuade the judge to give you the order you want. On the other hand, the law specifically says that if you were the full-time caretaker of your grandchild for some period of time, there is a stronger presumption that it will be good for your grandchild to see you regularly, and you are more likely to get the order.

You should realize that, although the law says you have the right to ask for visitation even if your grandchildren live together with both of their parents, it is difficult to get a court to overrule the parents' wishes. If a parent objects to your visiting your grandchild, the court is going to look very closely at the family relationship to decide what is in your grandchild's best interest. If there is any alternative, any way to persuade your son or daughter to arrange visitation without a court order, you should pursue that option. The courts are very reluctant to tell parents what to do with their children, even when the law recognizes your rights. This does not mean that you should not try to enforce your right to see your grandchildren; it just means that you should see a court proceeding as a last resort.

One option to consider before going to court is to participate in family counseling. Another option is mediation. Mediation is a process by which the various parties to a dispute sit down together with a third party (someone not involved) who acts as a referee while everyone talks about what should or can be done. Mediators are trained to help the parties reach agreement. They are not judges, and they will not tell you what you must do. The goal is for the parties to agree on a plan that satisfies everyone as much as possible. If you are not willing to go along with the agreement or you cannot reach agreement, you can end the mediation and go before a judge.

Parties to custody and visitation complaints are referred to mediation through the courts. There is no charge for this mediation service. Private mediation services are also available, and they can be a means of reaching agreement without filing a formal complaint. Some attorneys are trained mediators or can refer you to someone who can mediate. If you look in the phone book under "Mediation Services" you will find a list of private mediators who will work with you for a fee.

If the parents are in the process of getting a divorce and determining custody, you can intervene in the proceeding, meaning that you can become a party requesting visitation. If the parents are separated or divorced and custody has already been decided, you can file a request to amend the custody order. If the family is intact and there is no custody proceeding or final order, a complaint for visitation must be filed. Although it is possible to represent yourself in such a proceeding, you may want to hire an attorney to develop legal arguments based on case law. The more complicated the relationships and issues, the more reason to consider requesting the assistance of an attorney.

CUSTODY

Michelle's daughter is an alcoholic, and she does not take care of her child, Tommy. Michelle wants Tommy to live with her.

Michelle can request custody of Tommy. The court will first consider whether Tommy has a parent who can take care of him. If his mother is unable to provide proper care and his father is unavailable or also unfit, the court will consider who should have custody of Tommy. As his grandmother, Michelle will be considered, but she must be willing to be investigated to determine her fitness as a parent for Tommy. The court can order her to establish why she should have custody, including, in some cases, asking her to undergo a psychological examination, with a report to be provided to the court. The fact that

Michelle has already raised children and is Tommy's grandmother is helpful, but it will not control the court's decision.

UNDERSTANDING THE LAW. If the parents of your grandchild are unable to care for him or her, you may decide that you should seek custody. The law provides that if a parent is unfit or neglects a child, anyone with an interest in the child can file an action in Family Court to request custody (N.J.S.A. 9:2-7.1 et seq.). The court will have you investigated to determine whether to place the child in your care. The law gives preference to placing the child with you, a grandparent, rather than placing the child with someone who is not a family member. Even with this preference in your favor, you must still be found by the court to be the best placement for your grandchild.

When making a decision about whether you should have custody of your grandchild, the court will take into consideration your age and your potential ability to care for small children as you get older. The court will also consider your financial resources, the age of your grandchild, your health, and your history and fitness as a parent. You should consider whether you have the stamina that will be required to care for your grandchild.

If your son or daughter is unable to care for your grandchild, he or she could also voluntarily give you temporary or permanent custody. If you are named the legal guardian, you can avoid the formalities and possible hostility of a court proceeding. But this may not give you the security and permanence of a court determination. If your son or daughter decides to request that the child be returned to him or her and you disagree with this request, you will have to defend the arrangement in court. The court will always try to determine the best interest of the child.

11. Divorce and Remarriage

IS DIVORCE AN ELDER LAW ISSUE?

Why, you may ask, is there a discussion of divorce in a book about elder law? For two reasons. As couples go through life changes such as retirement, they sometimes find that conflicts that were buried or less significant take on new importance, and they feel that divorce is the answer. Sometimes long-term resentments come to the forefront, and one party is no longer willing to tolerate behaviors that were considered forgivable earlier. The second reason is that some couples may, rightly or wrongly, feel that divorce is the best response to some financial difficulties. For example, the need to divide property after a divorce may seem to protect one spouse from the potential impoverishment of paying for nursing home care.

If conflicts and differences cause an individual or couple to consider divorce, it is up to the individual or the couple to decide what is best. It is worth considering whether counseling or advice from a professional could resolve your differences. If financial choices make divorce seem appealing, make sure your understanding of the consequences is correct. It would be wise to consult with an attorney or financial advisor about alternative strategies before taking the step of filing for a divorce.

> *Thomas and Velma have been married for many years. They reside together in the house in which Thomas grew up, where they raised their children. The marriage has never been easy, and they fight often. After a terrible fight, Thomas left the house. When he returned, Velma told him that she was going to court to obtain a restraining order to keep him out of the house and that she wanted a divorce. Thomas agrees that they should get a divorce, but he does not want her to be able to stay in the house, and he does not think that there should be a restraining order against him, since he has not harmed Velma. He is concerned about his reputation, but most of all he is concerned that he not lose the house in a divorce, since it has been in his family for many years.*

A restraining order is a court order requiring one party to stay away from the other. It is obtained when one party claims that the other has

DOMESTIC VIOLENCE

If you are a victim of domestic violence, you can obtain a court order prohibiting the abuser from committing any further acts of violence against you and from having any future contact with you. Contact your local women's shelter or crisis intervention agency for assistance. The domestic violence law applies to you if you are hurt or threatened by, among others, your spouse or former spouse, someone who lives with you, or someone you date.

It is not difficult to get this type of court order. Go to the Family Court at your county courthouse during regular business hours. During evenings and on weekends and holidays you can apply for this type or order through your local police department. You can also file criminal charges if you want.

When you apply for an order, you will be granted a temporary restraining order prohibiting the abuser from committing any violent acts against you or even contacting you. Once you have this order, the Family Court will hold a hearing within ten days to determine if the restraining order should be permanent. At the hearing the court will consider the person's history of physical violence and may also consider any history of psychological, emotional, or economic abuse.

In addition to ending the violence and keeping the abuser away from you, a temporary or final restraining order may require, among other things, that the abuser leave the house or apartment, even if the lease or the house deed is in the abuser's name; pay you support; pay for costs that resulted from the domestic violence, such as the costs of repairing damage to your house; pay your attorneys' fees; and receive counseling.

If you know someone who is a victim of domestic violence but who is not physically or mentally capable of applying for a restraining order, the law provides that you can apply for a temporary restraining order on the victim's behalf.

been abusive and is intended to prevent future violence by keeping the parties separated. If the party against whom the order is entered violates it by approaching the one who obtained the order, whether by going to the house or by following him or her on the street, the police can arrest the person for violating the order. In this case, Velma would have to go to court and argue that Thomas's behavior violated the law and she is in danger. Thomas can oppose the entry of a restraining order against him. If he has not hit Velma or damaged any property, there is no reason for an order to be entered. Their arguing and Velma's wanting him out of the house are probably not enough to require a restraining order.

Obtaining a divorce will require filing a court action and either agreeing to a distribution of property or having the court order distribution. New Jersey law requires either that there be a fault basis for divorce, such as cruelty or that there be a lengthy separation during which Thomas and Velma live apart. New Jersey uses a strategy known as "equitable distribution" to divide property, which is intended to make a fair determination of who should obtain what property when a marriage ends. If Thomas and Velma cannot agree on how the property they own should be divided, a judge will consider what property was acquired during the marriage, the financial circumstances of each party, the length of the marriage, and what is fair. If Thomas wants to be certain he will get the house, he might want to work out the property division with Velma before they go to court so that they will each get what they want.

UNDERSTANDING NEW JERSEY DIVORCE LAW. Obtaining a divorce requires filing a court action that asserts a reason for divorce that is recognized in the New Jersey divorce statute (N.J.S.A. 2A:34-1 et seq.). Eight different reasons for divorce are recognized. There is only one "no fault" basis for divorce: that the couple has lived apart for eighteen months and there is no hope of reconciliation. All other claims involve assigning blame to one party, and some of these require that a specific amount of time has passed before they can be used. For example, if you allege cruelty in a complaint for divorce, the statute states that you cannot file the complaint until three months after the "last act of cruelty complained of in the complaint."

In addition to separation for eighteen months and cruelty, possible grounds for divorce include adultery, desertion for twelve or more

---

RESIDENCY REQUIREMENTS FOR DIVORCE

In most cases one spouse must have been a resident of New Jersey for at least one year in order to file a divorce action in the New Jersey courts. If the case involves allegations of abuse, the residency requirement is waived, and the only requirement is that one spouse be a New Jersey resident at the time that the divorce action is filed.

---

months, addiction to narcotics or alcoholism for twelve or more months, institutionalization for mental illness for two or more years, imprisonment for eighteen or more consecutive months, and voluntary deviant sexual conduct without the consent of the plaintiff (the one bringing the complaint).

A judgment of divorce will include a decision on distribution of property and alimony, if it is requested.

EQUITABLE DISTRIBUTION OF PROPERTY. In a divorce action the court will attempt to divide all the property you own, including real estate and personal property, in a manner that is fair to both parties. In order to do this the judge will consider how all the property was acquired, because the court can divide only what you earned or purchased during the marriage, and it will not divide property that was a gift or an inheritance.

To decide what would be a fair division of your property, the court will consider a long list of factors, including how long you were married, each spouse's age and health, your standard of living, each spouse's income and earning capacity at the time of the divorce, your debts, what property you brought to the marriage, and what you contributed to the marriage through earnings or as a homemaker.

One asset that can be difficult to divide in a divorce is a pension. Since the value of a pension is tied to the length of the employee's life, it is difficult to put a current value on a pension, but it can be done by an actuary. By using life expectancy, a value can be determined and the amount can then be divided. If this is done, the pension cannot also be counted as income when deciding alimony.

ALIMONY. If you request support from your spouse after your divorce, the court will consider awarding alimony in addition to distributing property. There are two different kinds of alimony: permanent alimony and rehabilitative alimony. Permanent alimony is intended to last as long as necessary to provide continuing income to one spouse. It ends when the recipient marries again or when either spouse dies. Rehabilitative alimony, on the other hand, is intended to last for a certain period of time. For example, it might be awarded to allow one spouse to go to school to learn job skills, and it would be expected to end when that spouse was able to get a job.

To decide whether alimony is necessary and what amount should be awarded, the court will again look at a list of factors, including the requesting party's need for income and the ability of the other party to pay, the number of years the parties have been married, their ages and health, their ability to support themselves, their ability to get a job or to get training to help them get a job, and how the marital property has been divided. If a share of a retirement benefit is divided as marital property, the income it produces after distribution will not be taken into consideration in deciding alimony.

If you are receiving permanent alimony and you remarry, you are no longer entitled to receive it. If at the time you remarry your former spouse owes you alimony that was not paid on time, you can still receive what is owed. If the award of alimony was rehabilitative, you may still be entitled to receive it after you remarry, depending on the circumstances of the award. An award of rehabilitative alimony can generally be modified if circumstances change. In the case of either type of alimony, if your former spouse dies, you are no longer entitled to receive alimony. In order to meet your needs, the court can require your former spouse to maintain life insurance for your benefit.

PAYMENT OF ATTORNEY FEES. The court can order your spouse to pay the fees you pay your attorney to obtain a divorce if this is reasonable. The court will consider your financial circumstances and those of your spouse in making this decision, as well as what legal services have been needed. This decision can be made at the end of the case, or it can be made at the beginning if this is necessary for you to hire an attorney.

SOCIAL SECURITY BENEFITS AFTER DIVORCE. If you were married for at least ten years before your divorce, you can receive Social

Security benefits based on your former spouse's earnings record, even after the end of your marriage. If you are at least sixty-two years old and are not eligible for an equal or higher benefit based on your own earnings or someone else's earnings (those you receive as a widow or widower, for example), you are entitled to claim benefits based on your former spouse's earnings. This will not affect the amount of benefits your former spouse receives, and he or she cannot prevent you from receiving these benefits. It does not matter if your former spouse has remarried as long as you are single. If you have remarried, you can claim benefits based on your former spouse's record only if your current spouse receives benefits as a widow, widower, parent, or disabled child. For more information, see chapter 1 on Social Security benefits.

You may also be entitled to survivors' benefits even after divorce. After your former spouse's death, you are entitled to survivors' benefits if you were married for at least ten years and you are over sixty years old (or fifty if you are disabled), if you are not eligible for an equal or higher benefit based on your own earning record, and if you are not currently married or you remarried after age sixty.

REMARRIAGE

If you decide to marry again after divorcing or being widowed, you should consider whether a premarital agreement is appropriate for you. A premarital agreement, also known as a prenuptial agreement, records the decisions that you and your future spouse have made regarding property and living expenses in the event of death or divorce. It can include provisions for ownership and control of property, alimony, wills, and life insurance beneficiaries.

If you have children or grandchildren and you want to be sure certain property goes to them, you can make provisions for this in a written prenuptial agreement signed prior to your marriage. If you think a premarital agreement is appropriate for you, consult with an attorney.

You should also review your will to ensure that your children will receive the property you intend them to have. Depending on the provisions of your will, your remarriage may affect your distribution scheme. Remember that your spouse is entitled to a share of your estate even if he or she is not named in your will (see chapter 6).

12. Abuse of the Elderly

After being hospitalized for several weeks, Clare was no longer able to live on her own. Her niece, Joanne, offered to take care of her, and Clare moved into Joanne's apartment. She is not happy there, and she feels that Joanne is limiting her contact with other family members, but she has nowhere else to live. When Clare asks Joanne questions about her Social Security checks, Joanne says, "Just worry about getting better" or "There's enough money for what you need," but she never gives Clare any money or answers her questions directly.

Clare is sure that Joanne is taking her checks and spending the money on herself. She thinks Joanne may even have arranged for Social Security to send the checks to her directly instead of depositing them in Clare's bank account. Joanne asked Clare to sign some legal documents, saying that they would make things "easier for both of us," and Clare did not feel as if she could refuse. She is pretty sure that one of the papers was a power of attorney. Once when she told Joanne she wanted to move out, Joanne grabbed her hard enough to leave bruises on her arm and yelled at her. Later she told Clare not to think any more about living on her own, and said she would always take care of her. Clare is very unhappy, but she does not know where she would live if Joanne did not take care of her.

This is a story that presents a problem with no easy solution. Joanne is taking financial advantage of Clare, taking her Social Security checks, and gaining access to Clare's property by having her sign legal documents Clare does not understand. Bruising Clare and yelling at her to dissuade her from leaving are abusive acts. However, Clare may not want to live elsewhere, may feel dependent on Joanne, and may not have an alternate place to live if she does not want to move into a nursing home.

LEGAL ISSUES

Criminal statutes outlaw assault and violence, including domestic violence. If you are hurt or threatened by someone who lives with you or has lived with you in the past, you are protected by the Prevention of

---

CALL FOR HELP

If you are concerned that you or a family member or friend is being abused or exploited, contact Adult Protective Services by calling (800) 792-8820. This agency will send someone to visit you or the person about whom you are concerned and determine whether the person is in need of services.

Domestic Violence Act. This law allows you to get an order from the court requiring your abuser to stay away from you. In addition, New Jersey has a statute that specifically prohibits endangering the welfare of people who are elderly or disabled. This statute makes it a crime to neglect a vulnerable person or to fail to permit any act necessary for the physical or mental health of a person who is elderly or disabled. The Adult Protective Services Act defines and provides services to intervene and prevent abuse, exploitation, and neglect of vulnerable adults.

Together these laws, which are described in this chapter, prohibit and attempt to prevent not only abuse of the elderly, but exploitation by those who care for them. It is a violation to fail to provide food or medical care, but it is also a violation to take on the care of a vulnerable adult and then use his or her benefits checks for one's own benefit without the consent or understanding of the person in one's care. A vulnerable adult is entitled to protective services to ensure that he or she receives the care that is needed. In addition, "endangering the welfare of an elder" is a crime that can subject the abuser to criminal penalties.

UNDERSTANDING THE LAW

Both the Prevention of Domestic Violence Act and the Adult Protective Services Act are intended to provide remedies for those who are being hurt or exploited by family members, caretakers, or others with whom they have a relationship. Criminal punishment is given for endangering the welfare of an elder. These laws cover different problems and provide different remedies, so if there is a problem there may be several ways to solve it.

THE PREVENTION OF DOMESTIC VIOLENCE ACT

The Prevention of Domestic Violence Act (N.J.S.A. 2C:25-17 et seq.) covers abuse in a number of circumstances. If you are hurt or threatened by your spouse, former spouse, someone with whom you have a child, any other present or former member of your household, or someone who you are dating you are protected by this statute. If the actions of this person make you afraid for your safety, you can get help. By going to the county courthouse—or, if the courthouse is closed or you are unable to get to the courthouse, by contacting the police—you can obtain a restraining order.

Once you file a complaint, a judge will issue a temporary restraining order that will prevent your abuser from coming to your house and will require that the abuser stay away from you. If the abuser violates the order, you should call the police. Once the restraining order has been served, the police must arrest the abuser if he or she violates the restraining order. At the time the temporary restraining order is issued, the court will set a date for a final restraining order hearing to determine if the restraining order should become permanent. It is important to follow up on the initial order and appear at the final order hearing, or the restraining order will be dismissed.

You do not have to have an attorney to obtain a restraining order. The statute is designed to allow you to protect yourself without needing a lawyer. But be prepared to prove to the judge why you are afraid and what your abuser has done that has hurt or threatened you. Witnesses and photographs of bruises or injuries can be very helpful. Bring medical records and police reports with you to the final restraining order hearing.

Consider how you will protect yourself from your abuser, and also how you will care for yourself if your abuser has been giving you money or helping you care for yourself. You are entitled to ask the court for support from your abuser if you have been receiving it. But if the person who is hurting you has also been helping you, think about what you will do when he or she is no longer available. Is there someone else who will help out, another family member or a neighbor? There are community agencies that might be able to help so that you will not have to allow your abuser back into your home. Contact your county Office on Aging or a local domestic violence shelter.

In the example of Clare in our story, the fact that Joanne is taking money from Clare is not a reason to get a restraining order. But Joanne has hurt Clare and used threatening language, which might mean that a restraining order is appropriate. A restraining order would mean that Joanne would be required to leave the home, and Clare would need someone to care for her. Clare will have to decide whether she is afraid of more violence from Joanne. It might be more important to address the financial issues and determine whether there is somewhere better for Clare to live.

The Prevention of Domestic Violence Act is a civil statute intended to provide protection to victims of violence. There are two other statutes that might be more relevant to some circumstances of elder abuse: that entitled Endangering the Welfare of an Elderly or Disabled Person and the Adult Protective Services Act. These are criminal statutes.

ENDANGERING THE WELFARE OF AN ELDERLY OR DISABLED PERSON

Endangering the Welfare of an Elderly or Disabled Person (N.J.S.A. 2C:24-8) makes it a crime for someone with a duty to provide care for a senior to neglect or fail to permit any act necessary for the physical or mental health of that person. This means that someone who is responsible for caring for a senior must protect that person from harm and not take steps that will put him or her at risk. This is not limited to physical injury, but can also include taking money, which prevents the senior from being able to obtain needed medical care. This offense is a crime, so if you suspect someone of neglect, contact the police.

In the example from our story, Joanne seems to be providing the care Clare needs. If she is depriving Clare of medical care or fails to make sure there is food available that is appropriate to Clare's needs, she may be guilty under this statute. But the fact that she is taking Clare's money, even if she is not endangering her, can be addressed under the Adult Protective Services Act rather than Endangering the Welfare of an Elder.

THE ADULT PROTECTIVE SERVICES ACT

The Adult Protective Services Act (N.J.S.A. 52:27D-406 et seq.) established an Adult Protective Services agency in each county. These agencies investigate and address reports of abuse, neglect, or exploita-

---

CALL FOR HELP

If you have a concern about how you or a family member or friend is being treated in a nursing home or other long-term care facility, write the Office of the Ombudsman for the Institutionalized Elderly, P.O. Box 807, Trenton, NJ 08625-0807, or call (800) 792-8820. Complaints are taken 24 hours a day. Callers can remain anonymous, and reports are confidential.

---

tion of a vulnerable adult. A vulnerable adult is a person eighteen years of age or older who resides in a community setting and who, because of a physical or mental illness, disability, or deficiency, lacks sufficient understanding or the ability to make, communicate, or carry out decisions concerning his or her well-being and is the subject of abuse, neglect, or exploitation (N.J.S.A. 53:27D-407). If there are problems, the agency tries to provide services so that the vulnerable person will be properly cared for. It can arrange for counseling, visiting nurses, and other social services. If these services are sufficient, they may allow a senior who needs care to receive necessary services, prevent further abuse or exploitation, and allow the senior to avoid admission to a nursing home. If services cannot be provided to make the senior safe in his or her own home, Adult Protective Services has the power to take steps to institute a guardianship or to use other measures to protect the vulnerable senior. This can include forcing access to a senior even when the caretaker objects, making referrals for mental health services, and petitioning for guardianship or civil commitment.

If you or someone you know is being abused or endangered, reach out for assistance. There are services available, so tolerating a bad situation is not the only alternative. Clare in our story might be able to move to an assisted living facility where she will get the care she needs without losing her independence. But until she takes action, Joanne will be able to continue taking advantage of her.

ABUSE IN NURSING HOMES

The statutes already discussed are focused on preventing and addressing abuse in a private setting. But unfortunately nursing homes can also be settings for abuse. Patients can be victimized through physical or verbal abuse; misuse of restraints; neglect, including failing to provide proper medical care; and theft of personal property. See chapter 5 regarding nursing home selection criteria that help avoid abusive situations. If you believe that you or someone else is being abused, contact the Office of the Ombudsman for the Institutionalized Elderly (see box on page 113).

V. EMPLOYMENT, DISCRIMINATION, AND PENSIONS

This section provides information that will help you to identify employment discrimination and understand what you can do if an employer discriminates against you. It also looks at the law regarding pensions to help you understand your pension and avoid common problems.

Some typical questions that are addressed in this section are:

- If I get fired before I vest in my pension, is that age discrimination?
- Can my employer force me to retire?
- If I need a lighter workload because I have arthritis, can I make my employer adjust my duties?
- How do I file a discrimination complaint?
- If I need time off to care for my ill spouse, can I get my job back?
- Can I be sure I will get my full pension when I retire?
- What if my company goes bankrupt?
- If I have a 401(k) pension plan, do I have any protection if the money is mishandled?
- Can I get unemployment benefits and my pension if I get laid off?

13. Employment and Discrimination

"I would be happy to work, but no one wants older workers." This is a statement often made by older clients. You might get the sense that there is no place in the workforce for you after a certain age. But it is important to know your rights to obtain or to keep employment without regard to your age. An additional issue is whether disability, which might come with age, prevents you from working. Efforts to see that those who have the ability to work are given an opportunity to do so have led to the passage of two federal laws and related state laws that you should know about. The Age Discrimination in Employment Act and the Americans with Disabilities Act are both designed to protect you from losing your job when you still have the ability to work. The New Jersey Law Against Discrimination also protects you from discrimination based on age or disability.

AGE DISCRIMINATION

Bob is fifty-five years old and has worked for the Bigg Company for twelve years. In a recent round of layoffs he was told that his position was being eliminated, and he is now unemployed. A few weeks after his layoff, in a conversation with a former coworker who is still at the Bigg Company, Bob was told that John, his former assistant, is now filling his position. John is forty-three years old. Bob believes that his employer wanted to get rid of all of the more senior employees in order to save money by replacing them with lower-salaried workers.

This situation falls under the Age Discrimination in Employment Act (ADEA). If Bob was replaced by a younger worker, he can argue that he lost his job due to age discrimination and sue his former employer to get his job back and for lost wages. The ADEA protects all workers over forty years old, so both Bob and the worker who replaced him, John, are covered by the act. The question that a court or agency considering Bob's complaint will have to decide will be what role age discrimination played in his former employer's decisions. It is illegal to fire a worker because of his or her age, but it is not illegal to choose a lower-salaried worker over a better-paid worker. So Bob can win a suit if the Bigg Company based its decisions on age, but not if it decided for economic reasons to lay off Bob and keep John.

UNDERSTANDING THE LAW. The Age Discrimination in Employment Act (29 U.S.C. sec. 621 et seq.) is a federal statute designed to address age discrimination. It covers anyone over forty years old, and it applies to "employers, labor organizations, or employment agencies." In order to be considered an employer under this law a business must be large enough to meet the definition in the statute. Basically, the business must have twenty or more employees for at least twenty calendar weeks a year. So a small business, such as a shop with twelve employees, would not be covered by this law, and an employee of that shop who lost his or her job would not be able to sue under the ADEA to get that job back.

An employer who fits this definition is prohibited from making employment decisions on the basis of age. The Bigg Company can conduct layoffs if it chooses, but it cannot decide to lay off only those employees who are over fifty. If an employee who is fired or laid off can establish that the Bigg Company based its decisions about which staff members to cut on an illegal reason, that employee or class of employees is entitled to return to their lost jobs and to receive back pay from the Bigg Company.

Also under this statute, an employer cannot require all employees to retire at a certain age. It can, however, use a seniority system, but not if the system forces older people out of work. There are certain exceptions to this provision. The law includes a list of types of employees for whom a mandatory retirement age is allowed. This list includes law enforcement officers, federal judges, commercial airline pilots, and certain executives with particular provisions for pension income. In addition to the positions that are named in the statute, certain other positions can be claimed by an employer to have being younger as a "bona fide occupational qualification (BFOQ)." It is difficult for employers to establish that age is a real qualification, but the law allows them to try.

The ADEA prohibits discrimination only on the basis of age. If the Bigg Company wants to fire all employees who have been with the company for more than eight years to prevent them from vesting in their pension benefits, the ADEA will not apply. This may be a discriminatory decision for a different reason (see the discussion of pensions later in this chapter), but it is not based on age, and therefore a court will not use the ADEA to punish the employer.

FILING A COMPLAINT

To file a complaint, write to the New Jersey Division of Civil Rights at 140 East Front Street, 6th Floor, P.O. Box 089, Trenton, NJ 08625-0089, or call (609) 292-4605, or write to the Equal Employment Opportunity Commission at 1801 L Street NW, Washington, DC 20507, or call (202) 663-4900.

FILING A COMPLAINT. If you believe that you have a valid claim under the ADEA, you should act quickly to file. You have about eight months (240 days) from the time you lose your job or are otherwise discriminated against to begin the complaint process. You file a complaint with the New Jersey Division on Civil Rights or with the federal Equal Employment Opportunity Commission (EEOC). To file you can either complete a form explaining your complaint or write a letter and have it notarized. Your complaint should be specific. Describe what happened and who did what. State any particular actions that you think were discriminatory and why you think the employer discriminated against you.

The agency with which you file will investigate your complaint and attempt to settle it with your employer, or it will decide not to act in your case and issue you a "right to sue" letter. This letter simply demonstrates that the agency will take no further action; it does not affect the merits of your case. You cannot file a complaint in court until you receive this letter. If the Division on Civil Rights or the EEOC does not resolve your case, do not feel that is the end of the matter. These agencies resolve only a small fraction of the cases that are brought to them. They are responsible for cases alleging any kind of illegal discrimination in employment, including discrimination on the basis of race, sex, religion, and disability, and they do not have the resources to pursue every case.

WAIVERS OF THE RIGHT TO SUE. It is important to note that an employer is permitted to ask an employee to sign a waiver of his or her rights under the ADEA. For example, an employer can offer you an early retirement package that is conditioned on signing such a waiver.

FINDING A LAWYER TO HELP YOU

The National Employment Lawyers Association can refer you to a New Jersey lawyer with experience in employment discrimination cases. For a list of New Jersey members, send a written request with a stamped, self-addressed envelope to the National Employment Lawyers Association at 600 Harrison Street, Suite 535, San Francisco, CA 94107. Telephone and fax requests will not be accepted. Information only is available on the association's web site at www.nela.org.

If you accept the retirement package and sign the waiver, you are agreeing not to later claim you were discriminated against under the ADEA. This might be an attractive option if the alternative is to be laid off without the additional benefits of the package. You should understand that this waiver is valid under the law and you will not be able to sue your employer if it meets certain requirements:

- It must be written.
- Your acceptance must be knowing and voluntary.
- You must be getting something in exchange for signing (such as extra benefits in an early retirement package).
- You must be advised to consult an attorney.
- You must be given at least twenty-one days to consider the agreement.

If you are offered such a waiver and you think that you might have a valid claim under the ADEA, consult an attorney before you sign. Retaining your right to sue under the ADEA may be valuable, but you should evaluate the time, stress, and risk involved in suing against the likelihood of success. An attorney with experience in this area can help you to determine what you can anticipate.

DISABILITY DISCRIMINATION

Greg was diagnosed with lung cancer a year ago. He has continued to work during treatment, and he had enough sick days available that he has not had to ask for any additional time off. He says he is a little slower at getting work done than before, but that he is still doing everything he always did. Recently he was assigned a new supervisor, and the new boss told him that he should consider retiring. Because of some comments he overheard the supervisor making to another employee, Greg thinks that if he does not retire he will be fired. The supervisor said that he thought Greg was trying to do too much and that anyone with lung cancer should "give himself and everyone else a break." He said that Greg was very slow and was "not keeping up."

Greg is covered by the Americans with Disabilities Act (ADA) (42 U.S.C. Sec. 12101 et seq.), and he should be able to stay in his job if he does not want to retire. Even though Greg is probably not disabled, since he can still do everything he could do before, the supervisor seems to perceive him as having a disability. There is nothing about lung cancer itself that should require Greg to retire if he does not choose to do so, but if the supervisor thinks that it makes him unable to do his job, he is being treated as if he had a disability. This is illegal.

If his lung cancer makes it difficult for Greg to do some things he could do more easily before, such as lifting and carrying boxes, he might be able to use the ADA to require his employer to make adjustments to his job description so he can continue working. If this is the case, Greg is claiming that he is disabled because his cancer has limited his ability to perform some major life activities, such as breathing and doing physical work. If he is disabled his employer must make adjustments to activities that are not essential to his job. If lifting and carrying are small parts of the work he does, his employer should make other arrangements for these parts of the job to be done. But if lifting and carrying are at the heart of the job, Greg will not be entitled to keep his job. The goal of the ADA is to prevent someone like Greg from losing his job when a minor adjustment would make it possible for him to keep working. But an employer is not required to pay an employee who cannot do his or her job.

UNDERSTANDING THE LAW. If you have a disability or if your employer considers you disabled even if you do not have a disability, you are protected by the Americans with Disabilities Act, as well as the parallel provisions of the New Jersey Law against Discrimination (N.J.S.A. 10:5-1 et seq.). The intent of this law is to require an employer to make accommodations so that you can continue to work even if you are

FILING ADA AND SOCIAL SECURITY DISABILITY CLAIMS

If you think you have been discriminated against on the basis of a disability and you also think you are eligible for Social Security disability benefits (see chapter 1), you should consult an attorney before you file for benefits. Disability benefits are awarded when you are found to be unable to do any work. ADA claims are based on an argument that you could work if you received some accommodation from your employer. While it is possible to make both arguments successfully, it is important to be careful about what you say. An attorney can help you make the strongest possible arguments.

disabled. So if you experience some increasing disability as you age, you should consider whether this statute applies to you.

The ADA will protect you if your employer has more than fifteen employees; if you work for a very small company the law does not cover you. But if your employer is large enough the ADA applies if you are disabled, if you have a history of disability, or if you are perceived to be disabled. If you are disabled you must have an impairment severe enough to have a significant impact on your ability to do things such as walk, breath, see, or work. For example, if arthritis increasingly affects your ability to type, it will have to be severe enough to be found to substantially limit your ability to do a number of things before you will be considered disabled. If it is just that you find typing uncomfortable, you are probably not protected by the statute. Your impairment must have a major effect on your life, and it must also last for a long time. Even something severe is not a disability under the act if it is temporary, such as a broken bone.

FILING A COMPLAINT. The mechanics of filing an ADA complaint and what you should do are the same as for filing an age discrimination complaint. See the section above on the ADEA. It is important that you file within the statutory time limits, so if you think you are being discriminated against contact the New Jersey Division on Civil Rights or the Equal Employment Opportunity Commission quickly. If you want to consult with an attorney, the National Employment Lawyers Association can provide you with the names of New Jersey lawyers who handle employment cases (see the box in the section on the ADEA). Ask any attorney you contact what experience he or she has with the ADA so you can hire someone with expertise in this area.

THE FAMILY AND MEDICAL LEAVE ACT

If you need to take time off from your job for medical reasons or to care for a member of your immediate family (your spouse, child, or parent), your job is protected. The Family and Medical Leave Act (29 U.S.C.A. 2601–2654) gives you the right to take twelve weeks of unpaid leave in any twelve-month period. If you qualify you may take this time off and be assured that when you return you can go back to your job or to an equivalent job with equivalent pay, benefits, and other terms. Note that you can take this leave only to care for yourself or an immediate family member, not for more distant family members or for someone who is not your spouse.

In order to get this benefit you must work for a public employer or a business with fifty or more employees. You must also have worked for the employer for at least one year and have worked sufficient hours (1,250 hours over twelve months) and at a large enough location. If you work at a small branch of a large employer, there must be at least fifty employees within seventy-five miles for you to be entitled to this leave.

You are entitled to keep your health coverage while you are on leave, under the same terms as when you are employed. If you pay part of the cost while you work, you must continue to pay the same amount while you are on leave. If you tell your employer that you will not be returning to work, your employer no longer has to hold your job and you must switch to continuation health coverage to keep your health insurance.

14. Pensions

Rachel works for Cape Textiles as a secretary. The company encourages employees to contribute to the company-sponsored 401(k) retirement fund by offering to match a percentage of the dollars each employee commits to the fund. Rachel has taken advantage of this offer and contributes 8 percent of her salary to the fund. She plans to retire in a few years, and she will then draw on the fund to supplement her Social Security retirement benefits.

When Rachel began working for Cape Textiles she received regular statements about her 401(k) fund, but she paid little attention to what was in the statements. Recently she realized that there have not been any statements for a while. When she asked the employee in charge of benefits about the statements, she was assured that they were "in the works" and would appear shortly. There have not been any new statements for over a year. Now Rachel has heard rumors that Cape Textiles is going into bankruptcy, and she is concerned about her job and about her pension.

Rachel is right to be concerned. The fact that there have not been any statements recently is an indication that the company might not be handling the funds properly. Some companies have used retirement funds to try to solve financial problems. If Cape Textiles is insolvent and has already spent money that should have been invested in the 401(k) plan, Rachel and other employees may find that their investments are nonexistent. Although Rachel owns the funds already invested in the plan, if the company did not make the contributions it committed to making (both the funds withheld from her paycheck and the company's matching funds) she will have trouble getting the money she expected.

UNDERSTANDING THE LAW

Employers are not required to have pension plans, but if an employer offers a plan it must comply with the law. The plan must not be discriminatory, and employees are entitled to receive information so they will know their rights. Most employer plans are covered by the Employee Retirement Income Security Act of 1974 (ERISA). Govern-

124

ment employees and railroad employees are covered by different statutes.

A traditional pension was what is known as a "defined benefit" plan. An employer agreed to pay each employee a certain percentage of his or her salary after retirement if the employee worked for the company for a certain number of years. Most people who stayed with one employer for the required time received what they had been promised. Sometimes companies did not put aside enough money to pay the benefits they had committed to former employees, and then they went into bankruptcy and failed to pay the pensions. In order to protect these retirees, in 1974 the United States government passed the Employee Retirement Income Security Act (29 U.S.C.A. Sec. 1001 et seq.) to require more protection for employees, and it also established the Pension Benefit Guaranty Corporation to provide a pension guarantee to employees.

The Pension Benefit Guaranty Corporation works much as does the Federal Deposit Insurance Corporation (FDIC), which insures bank deposits, collecting premiums in order to have funds to cover companies that go under and cannot pay the pensions they have promised. But because of the burdens of the pension requirements in ERISA, many companies have shifted from the traditional defined benefit plan to a "defined contribution" pension plan. This term refers to retirement plans that are based on the amount of money put in by the company. The company agrees to provide retirement funds as a percentage of an employee's salary, but once the company has made its contribution the funds belong to the employee, and the company is not responsible for investing the money, ensuring the amount of money the employee will actually receive in retirement, or ensuring that that amount will be sufficient to last for the length of the employee's retirement.

There are different types of defined contribution plans. Cape Textiles (the employer of Rachel in our story) offers a 401(k) plan. The name refers to the section of the IRS (Internal Revenue Service) law that governs retirement plans of this type. There are several other kinds of defined contribution benefit plans, such as profit-sharing plans or employee stock ownership plans (ESOPs). They all work in essentially the same way.

The money belongs to the employee, and it is up to the employee to make investment decisions. Therefore, the employee bears the risk to invest wisely, to provide sufficient funds, and to determine how the

---

YOUR RIGHTS UNDER ERISA

The federal law that governs pensions, ERISA, gives you rights to receive information and to challenge decisions you think are unfair. You have the right to receive complete information about your pension plan, and if you challenge a decision you have the right to receive a decision in writing within a certain number of days.

---

funds are managed. A defined contribution plan gives more responsibility and more risk to the employee. The employee has to determine how much money is needed for retirement, how to make the money last, and how to invest it.

The company is responsible only for providing matching funds and choosing the plan through which the employee is investing. But there is still room for the employee to be at risk from mismanagement by the company. If the company does not put the money into the plan as it is supposed to, the money is not yet within the employee's control. So if money is withheld from each paycheck but the company sends money to the plan administrator only every three months, there is time when the money is within the control of the company to use for other purposes, and theoretically to lose on bad business decisions. New regulations require the company to turn over the money to the plan administrator more quickly, but enforcement may be difficult. It is also possible for a company not to make the contributions to the fund administrator for some period of time and use the cash for other things; some employees have found out too late that their employer was trying to shore up a shaky business by using these funds, and if the business fails the money may be unrecoverable.

This risk requires an employee with a defined contribution or 401(k) plan to be vigilant in understanding how the plan works and paying attention to the information provided to them. If statements stop coming or do not reflect the proper contributions, ask questions and find out if your company is misusing your retirement funds. There is no insurance for this type of pension, so the funds will not be made up by the government as they would be if invested in a defined benefit plan.

UNEMPLOYMENT BENEFITS AND PENSIONS

If you are laid off from your job and are entitled to unemployment benefits, you should realize that any pension you receive will affect the amount of the benefits you will be allowed. The government assumes that someone who is receiving a pension is less likely to return to work than someone who does not have a pension, so unemployment benefits are less likely to have the intended effect of tiding you over during a job search. Therefore, the government will take your pension into consideration in determining your unemployment benefits and will consider the source of the pension.

For example, if you receive a company pension and you were not required to make contributions to the pension fund during your employment, the full amount of the pension will be deducted from your unemployment benefits. If both you and your employer contributed to the pension fund, half of the amount you receive from your pension each month will be deducted from the unemployment benefits you would otherwise have received. Only if your employer made no contributions and the pension was entirely funded by you will you receive your full unemployment benefits. If the pension is from Social Security and is based on your own work record, your unemployment benefits will not be reduced.

If you lose your job and receive a lump-sum payout of your pension before you become entitled to full pension rights, the lump sum will not affect the unemployment benefits you receive. But if your rights to a pension are not affected when you lose your job and you receive a lump-sum payout, it will be treated in the same way it would if you received the pension over time. The agency will prorate the lump sum over your life expectancy using actuarial tables and will then reduce your benefit by the amount you would be expected to receive each month. If your retirement funds are rolled over into another retirement plan in accordance with the tax rules, this will not affect your unemployment benefits.

If you might be eligible for unemployment benefits, you should contact your local unemployment agency and apply. But you will have to disclose any pension payments you are receiving or any retroactive payments you receive, and this may reduce your benefits. If the amount of your unemployment benefits is more than the amount of the pension that will be subtracted, you will still receive any benefits to which you are entitled.

BENEFITS AND RETIREMENT

Along with a pension you may be receiving medical benefits from your former employer. Perhaps the company promised you that your medical coverage would remain the same for the rest of your life, but now you have received a letter saying that current economic circumstances have forced the company to cut back, and in the future you will have to pay a portion of the premiums and some co-payments, so your medical costs will go up. Is this permissible?

Unfortunately, this practice appears to be allowed under ERISA. Although there are many restrictions on what employers can do, the courts decided, in a case in which General Motors reneged on written promises to provide free medical care, that employers do not have to honor their agreements to provide medical care. Although there may be changes in this decision in the future, for now you must assume that your former employer can decide not to provide the same level of benefits as it promised to do at the time you retired. If you encounter this problem, you should check with an attorney to determine whether the law has been changed.

VI. CONSUMER ISSUES AND FRAUD

You have been a consumer all your adult life. Is there anything new you should know as you age? Some of what is addressed in the following chapters applies equally to consumers of any age, but some is particularly relevant to older consumers. The unfortunate fact is that many consumer frauds are directed at the elderly. This is true partly because many seniors have savings at their disposal, which makes them tempting targets. It is true also because some seniors are vulnerable because they are unfamiliar with handling their own finances or because increasing disability makes them easily confused or gullible. Aging leads some of them to consider different types of purchases, such as purchases of funeral contracts, that are subject to fraud or are difficult to understand sufficiently.

For all these reasons you should read the following chapters and consider what you can do before a problem arises. The more you know about scams that are being used to defraud people, especially those used against the elderly, and the more you know about your rights as a consumer, the less likely it is that someone can take advantage of you. If you ask for help before there is a problem, you can avoid the difficulty, stress, and loss of money that accompany many consumer problems.

The following chapters consider fraud schemes involving consumer rights and home repair contracts, including mortgage loans. They also consider fraud against the elderly, such as telephone fraud, mail fraud, and funeral fraud. Questions that are addressed include the following:

- Can I cancel a contract that I have signed?
- I am dissatisfied with the work performed by workmen under a home improvement contract. What should I do?
- Should I prepay for my funeral?
- How can I find out if an offer I received in the mail is legitimate?
- I ordered something by mail two months ago and still have not received it. What can I do?

15. Home Repair Contracts and the Consumer Fraud Act

Earl needed work done on his roof, so when a salesman came to his door and said that he was from XYZ Roofing, Earl invited him to come in and discuss what could be done. The salesman, whose name was Jimmy, told Earl that workers from XYZ could get the job done quickly, and they would use the best-quality materials. When Earl asked about the cost, Jimmy said the company would arrange financing and all Earl had to do was sign some papers. Earl could use his house as security for a loan. The whole job could be paid for at $280 a month, which Earl thought he could afford. Jimmy filled out a lot of papers and showed Earl where to sign. He told Earl that the workers would be at his house the next day.

The following morning three workers showed up and began work on the roof. They spent two hours up on the roof and then told Earl that they were done and his roof was better than ever. Earl thought the job was done pretty quickly, but did not question the workers when they said everything was completed. He received a call from a bank later in the day asking if the work was done, and he said yes. The following month the bank sent him a coupon book and he began making monthly payments of $280. Three months later, during a big storm, the roof started to leak and Earl realized that his roof had not been repaired properly. He called XYZ to complain, but he got an answering machine and no one ever called him back.

Earl's story demonstrates many elements of consumer fraud. Providing shoddy home improvements and leaving the consumer with a large debt, usually secured by a mortgage on his or her home, is seen with distressing frequency. But several laws intended to protect consumers give Earl remedies he can use to try to get his money back and not have to continue paying the mortgage. Earl should contact an attorney who is familiar with these laws as soon as possible so that he can exercise his right to sue the contractor and the mortgage holder before he spends more money. The law gives him the right to sue and to ask for damages, including the release of the mortgage, if he did not get what he contracted for. Although you generally have to pay when you sign a contract for work to be done, if the law is not followed and you are hurt by this, the Consumer Fraud Act provides protection.

UNDERSTANDING THE LAW

When you buy something, whether you go to a store or a salesman comes to your house, the seller must follow the consumer laws. Particular rules apply to different kinds of transactions. The discussion in this chapter covers the rules most relevant to work done on your house. The next chapter discusses other types of consumer transactions.

THE CONSUMER FRAUD ACT

The New Jersey Consumer Fraud Act (N.J.S.A. 56:8-1 et seq.) protects consumers from fraudulent and deceptive practices. It covers a wide range of sales. It includes specific requirements regarding such things as posted refund policies, limits on "going-out-of-business" sales, and clear price marking and advertising. In addition, the act states that any sales practice that misrepresents, conceals, makes false promises, or otherwise deceives the consumer with the intent of getting him or her to buy something is a violation.

The New Jersey attorney general has the power to enforce the Consumer Fraud Act, but the law also provides that any individual who loses money because of a violation can sue to recover the money lost. When an individual sues to enforce this law, the court is instructed to award three times the damages sustained as well as attorney fees and costs. This means that you can get back three times as much money as you lost and that your attorney's fees will be paid by the other party. The fact that attorney fees will be paid makes it easier to find an attorney who will be willing to help you even if you do not have a lot of money.

THE HOME IMPROVEMENT PRACTICES REGULATIONS

When a contractor agrees to work on your house, as did the roofing company that contracted to fix Earl's roof in our story, the contractor must follow a series of administrative regulations called the New Jersey Home Improvement Practices Regulations. Although regulations do not have the same power as a statute, the contractor must follow them or the fact that a regulation was violated can be used to show that you

REQUIRED RECEIPT FOR
HOME REPAIR CONTRACTS

When the Door-to-Door Home Repair Sales Act applies to a contract, the law requires that the contractor give you two copies of a receipt that clearly states the following:

- The contractor's name and place of business
- A description of the goods and services sold
- The amount of money paid

The receipt must also include the following paragraph, exactly as it is worded here:

NOTICE TO OWNER: YOU MAY RESCIND THIS SALE PROVIDED THAT YOU NOTIFY THE HOME REPAIR CONTRACTOR OF YOUR INTENT TO DO SO BY CERTIFIED MAIL, RETURN RECEIPT REQUESTED, POSTMARKED NOT LATER THAN 5 P.M. OF THE THIRD BUSINESS DAY FOLLOWING THE SALE. FAILURE TO EXERCISE THIS OPTION, HOWEVER, WILL NOT INTERFERE WITH ANY OTHER REMEDIES AGAINST THE HOME REPAIR CONTRACTOR YOU MAY POSSESS. IF YOU WISH YOU MAY USE THIS PAGE AS NOTIFICATION BY WRITING "I HEREBY RESCIND" AND ADDING YOUR NAME AND ADDRESS. A DUPLICATE OF THIS RECEIPT IS PROVIDED BY THE HOME REPAIR CONTRACTOR FOR YOUR RECORDS.

were defrauded. If the contractor does not follow the regulations, he is committing an unlawful practice, which is a violation of the Consumer Fraud Act. So you have the right to sue and recover three times your damages under the act.

The regulations cover remodeling, altering, painting, repairing, and modernizing a residence. They include a number of specific requirements as to what the seller must tell the buyer, what must be included in the contract, and steps the seller must take, such as obtaining necessary building permits. One clear violation is evident in Earl's story: XYZ Roofing should not have started work until they had obtained permits. It is likely that other violations appear in the contract itself. These are facts that Earl can use to make his case against the roofing company and, by extension, against the bank that holds the mortgage on his house.

THE DOOR-TO-DOOR SALES ACT

When you go to a store to buy something you have a chance to think about whether you want to make the purchase, and you can leave the store if you change your mind. If a salesperson comes to the house, many people find it more difficult to say no or to get the salesperson to leave if they want time to think over the purchase. For this reason there is a separate law that covers purchases you make in your home. If someone comes to you to sell a product, you are given time to reconsider your purchase, and the law requires that you be given a notice describing your right to change your mind.

When what you are purchasing is home repairs, the law that covers these purchases is called the Door-to-Door Home Repair Sales Act. This law states that you have three days after you sign a home repair contract in which to decide that you do not want to make the purchase. If you do not receive the required notice, the three days do not begin until you get the notice. Since XYZ Roofing started work the day after Earl signed the contract with them, he did not get a chance to reconsider the contract. This is a violation of the law.

SIGNING A MORTGAGE TO PAY FOR REPAIRS TO YOUR HOME

One way to pay for home improvements is to sign a note that uses your house as security for the loan. This means that the lender can take your house if you fail to make payments as you agree in the note. Often contractors will offer to arrange financing in order to get you to sign a home repair contract. This financing is usually secured by your house. It is a mortgage, even if the contractor does not explain this.

Once you sign a note to pay over time for repairs, other laws are involved that give you additional rights and protections. The federal government protects borrowers through the Truth in Lending Act (15 U.S.C. Sec. 1601). This gives you the right to know the exact amount you will pay over the life of the loan, including interest and principal, before you sign. The Truth in Lending Act also gives you

ALTERNATIVES TO CONTRACTOR FINANCING

Consumers often agree to let a contractor arrange to finance a home improvement contract because they think they have no alternative. It might make more sense for you to arrange financing yourself, and here are a few suggestions:

- Consider a home equity loan. Although this is also a mortgage on your property, if you shop around you might be able to find a much lower interest rate than that associated with the financing offered through the contractor.
- If you need substantial work done or are in need of additional income and you own your home with little or no existing mortgage, you might qualify for a "reverse mortgage." See chapter 17 for information on this way to obtain cash from the equity in your home.
- You may be eligible for free or low-cost work on you home through a charitable or government program. Contact your county Office on Aging (see appendix A). Most counties have a program to make minor repairs, and many areas provide government-backed financing for major essential repairs, such as roof repairs.

the right to change your mind and get out of the contract, even after you have signed.

WHAT TO DO IF YOU HAVE QUESTIONS

If a contractor did not do work of the quality you expected or did not do the work for which you contracted—or if you find that you are paying more than you understood you would—contact an attorney. Your county Office on Aging (see appendix A) can tell you if free legal services are available. If not, contact your county Bar Association and request a referral. Since attorney fees are available under these statutes, some attorneys will accept cases without asking you for an advance payment.

HOW TO AVOID PROBLEMS IN THE FIRST PLACE

There are several steps you can take to avoid problems with contractors. Before you sign a contract to have work done on your home, consider the following:

- Do not allow yourself to feel pressured into agreeing to work you are not sure needs to be done. Some unscrupulous workers will come to your home and try to scare you into agreeing to have work done that does not really need to be done or, if it needs to be done, does not need to be done on an emergency basis. In other words, you have time to shop for the right contractor. Give yourself time to get other estimates, compare costs, and see if you are eligible for free or low-cost assistance.
- Choose a contractor carefully. Get several estimates, and make some phone calls to learn if a contractor you are considering is reputable. If there is a trade association in your area, it can refer you to members. Ask what the association requires of its members. The New Jersey Remodelers Association checks the credit, insurance, and record of complaints of each of its members and requires members to respond to complaints. Call (856) 365-6572. You can also call your county Office of Consumer Affairs or call the state Division of Consumer Affairs Action Line at (609) 292-6392. The Better Business Bureau will tell you if there have been complaints against a business.
- Consider more than just the price a contractor gives you. Choosing a reputable contractor who will do a good job is important. If the lowest price will not give you what you want, it may cost you a lot more in the long run than a price that includes everything you want. Get references and check them. Find out who will actually do the work on your home. Some big companies, such as Sears, subcontract work to local contractors. You want to know if the people actually doing the work will do a good job.
- As described earlier, you may have the right to change your mind and cancel a home improvement contract. There should also be time to review the completed contract and make sure you understand what is involved. You should know from the contract when work will begin and when it will be completed, what work is to be done, and what materials will be used. Make sure you get all this information before you sign the documents.

- Make sure you understand the documents you are asked to sign. If you have difficulty understanding what you are agreeing to, ask for help. Do not feel pressured to sign without having your questions answered. *Do not sign a blank contract.*
- Ask for copies of all the documents you sign. You have a right to receive a copy of the completed contract when you sign it, so if you are told it will be completed later you should not sign. Do not allow work to begin until you have the copies. Once work has begun, do not sign anything that states the work is done until, in fact, it is completed. Most major jobs, such as roofing jobs, require permits. A properly permitted job will be inspected by a government inspector who can tell you whether the work has been properly completed. Insisting that a contractor obtain the required permits protects you even when you are unable to personally inspect the work. It will be more difficult to say later that you are dissatisfied with the job if you sign a document saying everything was done to your satisfaction. Of course if problems arise later that you could not know about when you signed, such as your roof begins to leak during the next big storm, you cannot be expected to have seen the problems. But obvious problems should be addressed as soon as possible.

16. Consumer Purchases and Common Consumer Fraud Schemes

Almost every day you probably buy something. You get the product you expect, and all is well. But sometimes something goes wrong. Whether it is because of an accident or because someone is trying to get away with something does not really matter; the damage has been done. To solve such problems when they arise, it is important that you know your rights and the remedies available to you. The focus of this chapter is on avoiding consumer problems and handling them when they do occur.

> *Simon received a phone call one afternoon informing him that he had won a valuable prize—a trip to Florida. He was excited at the prospect of getting a vacation, and he willingly provided the caller with the information that he was told was necessary to validate his eligibility. It was only when he received his next bank statement and discovered that $1,200 had been removed from his checking account that he realized that he had been defrauded. The caller had gotten his checking account number and by contacting the bank with this information had received a check directly from the bank without Simon's knowing that a transaction was being made.*

Simon contacted an attorney, and the attorney believed that two things had gone wrong in this case: first, Simon had given out information that the caller had used to take advantage of him, and second, the bank had exceeded its authority by giving someone money from Simon's account without ever hearing directly from him. Once the lapse in the bank's procedure was pointed out, the attorney for the bank agreed to try to get Simon's money back. The company that had called Simon maintained that during the phone call he had agreed to purchase health supplies. The company agreed to refund most but not all of the money, sending Simon a check for $800. The bank agreed to make up half of the remaining loss, returning $200 to Simon's account. Although Simon might have pursued return of the remaining $200 by suing the company, this would not have been easy, since the company was located in Georgia. So Simon decided not to pursue the matter further.

TELEPHONE FRAUD

This case reflects a very real problem that affects a large number of elderly people—telephone fraud. As the number of legitimate sales made over the telephone grows every year, the multitude of fraudulent schemes perpetrated by people who also use the telephone grows, too. In many cases seniors are targeted. Seniors are tempting targets because they are often too polite to hang up the telephone on a persistent salesperson, they have substantial assets, and they may be eager for an investment that appears to offer a more lucrative return than their current fixed income. It is also estimated that only a small fraction of these frauds are reported because the victims are embarrassed, do not think that anything can be done, and do not know whom to contact to report what has happened.

The first rule in these matters is do not give out financial information to any caller you do not know. If you place the call, you should know who you are calling and have a number to call again if there is a problem. But if someone who is not known to you calls you, you do not have any assurance that the information you are given is correct. The second rule is carefully check out any offer that seems too good to be true. It is unlikely that any legitimate offer has to be committed to immediately, so take the time to ask for written confirmation, to ask for advice from trusted financial advisors or family members, and to do research to be sure you know what you are investing in. If a prize costs money to claim, you are running the risk that the prize is not worth the amount of money you spend.

MAIL FRAUD

"You have won a valuable prize!" "You have won a free trip!" "You have won a new car!" Mail bearing these and many similar statements arrives in your mailbox regularly. You are enticed to open the envelope, and the sender hopes that you will follow up by purchasing a product or calling for more information or agreeing to change your phone service in exchange for receiving your prize. Some of these offers are legitimate. But many of them are not, and they can be either misleading or fraudulent. How can you protect yourself? Be wary of any offers you respond to, and be particularly cautious if the offer of a prize or something free requires that you make a payment before your receive anything.

Typical of mail fraud schemes are postcards you receive in the mail offering you a prize. You read that by signing the enclosed postcard and sending it back you will qualify for a free hotel stay or some other prize. Only if you read the extremely small print over the signature line will you know that by signing you are agreeing to change your telephone long distance carrier. The carrier may charge considerably more than your existing service, and there may be a fee for changing services. The prize may either never appear or be virtually worthless, so you will receive nothing of value in exchange for the added telephone costs. You were given the information that your service would be changed, but it was given in print so small that you could easily miss it. You have cooperated in a scam.

The law requires that information be provided about what you are winning, and what service changes will be made. But the fact that the required information is provided may not be sufficient if you do not read extremely carefully. So be cautious whenever you think you are getting something for nothing. This may seem like very basic advice, but it is important to remember that mail fraud is big business, and these schemes continue because they work. People want to receive prizes and they agree to pay for products and services they do not want or cannot afford.

A similar problem arises when you are offered a prize for which you must pay a processing or handling fee. Chances are good that the prize is worth less than the fee you are paying, so the business is essentially selling you the prize, making you think you are getting something more. If you are putting up money, the "prize" is not free, and it may not be worth what you pay. Think before you send money. Ask questions if you believe you have been singled out for something special.

Similarly, some people send personal letters asking for assistance exchanging currency. The recipient is usually asked to allow his or her bank account to serve as some kind of conduit for foreign funds. The goal is to get you to reveal banking information when you think you are dealing with a needy individual. Just because a letter is handwritten does not mean it is not part of a fraudulent scheme; these letters can be computer generated and just look as if they are in the handwriting of an individual.

Ordering products by mail can be a safe and effective way to shop. But you should know your rights as a consumer when using the mail. The law requires that a mail order business deliver the goods you ordered within six weeks. If you were not informed in advance that delivery would take more than six weeks, the seller has to offer you a full refund or a substitute product if delivery is not made within that time frame. If the substitute is not acceptable to you, you are entitled to a full refund. If the seller cannot provide the goods you ordered within the six weeks allowed by law, you are not obligated to pay, and any money you have already paid must be returned.

GETTING HELP

First and foremost, try not to become a victim in the first place. Once you send money or sign an agreement, there may be little that can be done to get your money back. Often the person committing mail fraud is a sophisticated criminal. If you respond to one fraudulent scheme, your name will sometimes be sold and you will be subject to repeated fraudulent offers. But if you are victimized by mail fraud, there are both state and federal laws available to help you. For assistance contact the New Jersey Division of Consumer Affairs by writing to 124 Halsey Street, Newark, NJ 07102, or calling (973) 504-6200. The division's e-mail address is askconsumeraffairs@oag.lps.state.nj.us.

FUNERAL FRAUD

Michael was very upset at the time of his wife's sudden death. He made the funeral arrangements alone, without another family member present. He does not remember the details of his conversations with the funeral director, but when he received the final bill it included many expensive items he does not remember discussing. He thinks that the funeral home took advantage of his sorrow and ripped him off.

Unfortunately, if Michael signed a valid contract there may be little he can do. But the manner in which funeral services are sold is regulated by law. Michael was entitled to receive a price list and a copy of the contract at the time he made the funeral arrangements. Failing to provide this information is considered an unfair practice. If Michael can show that he was not given the required information, he can file a complaint with the New Jersey Board of Mortuary Science, which licenses funeral home

---

COMPLAINTS ABOUT FUNERALS

For complaints about funerals, do one of the following:

- Write the Board of Mortuary Science of New Jersey at P.O. Box 45009, Newark, NJ 07102, or call (973) 504-6425.
- Contact your local Better Business Bureau.
- Contact the regional Federal Trade Commission, which follows patterns of complaints. Write to the New York Regional Office of the Federal Trade Commission at 150 William Street, Suite 1300, New York, NY 10038, or call (212) 264-1207.
- Call Funeral and Memorial Societies of America (FAMSA) at (800) 765-0107, or e-mail them at www.funerals.org/famsa. This organization will assist you in determining where to direct a complaint, tell you whether you have a valid complaint, and help you negotiate with the funeral home or cemetery through its ombudsman program.

---

operators. Contact the Board of Mortuary Science by writing to 124 Halsey Street, Newark, NJ 07102, or calling (973) 504-6425.

Especially in the area of funerals, advance planning can make a big difference. Family members should consider what they do and do not want included in the services provided, and they should not agree to anything more. It is very difficult to make careful decisions when you are upset, and some funeral directors take advantage of this. That is why the regulations require that you receive a printed list of prices so you will know the cost of all the services you have requested. If you try to eliminate some services and you are told they are required by law, ask to see a copy of the relevant law or regulations.

One way to avoid this difficulty might be to prepay for a funeral so that you will have time to consider the various services and costs at a less stressful time. The difficulty of prepaying is that there are often hidden costs that may not be foreseeable, so the family members may not benefit in the way the decedent expected. Funeral homes and mortuaries are required to give you a copy of an itemized price list. Be

---

HOW TO GET WHAT YOU WANT

The best way to make sure you and your family get what you want
for a funeral is to do the following:

- Take your time. It is best to plan ahead. Even if you do not
  plan ahead, do not rush to make funeral arrangements. You
  still want to know what you will be paying for.
- Buy less than you may be inclined to. Do not feel as if you
  have to make expensive choices when there are lower-cost
  alternatives. Do not believe everything a salesman tells you.
  Misleading or incorrect information is often given about the
  properties of caskets, for example.
- Do not let yourself be bullied. Take a family member or
  friend along with you to a funeral home. Ask questions about
  whatever you are told is required, and make sure you know
  what is included in a price and what extra charges to expect.
  See if you can alter plans to avoid unnecessary expenses.

---

sure you get one. And be sure to get more information before you sign
a prepaid funeral contract. The American Association of Retired Persons (AARP) offers a booklet called *Prepaying Your Funeral*. Write to
AARP at 601 E Street NW, Washington, DC 20049. Even if you decide
not to prepay for your funeral, you can still shop around and make
advance plans. Giving your family instructions about your choices will
relieve them of the need to decide what you would want.

Be very cautious about paying in advance. Even though planning
ahead is strongly encouraged, paying ahead is more complicated. It is
sometimes a wise decision, and it can preserve funds for your funeral
when you become eligible for Medicaid. If you choose to prepay for
your funeral, you can purchase life insurance so that the benefit will
cover the cost of your funeral or deposit money in a prepaid funeral
trust set up by the funeral home of your choice. State regulations
dictate how a funeral home must handle such a trust. Keep in mind
that costs may increase between the time you make these arrangements
and your death. You should try to allow for this increase so your family

will not be faced with additional costs. If you place money in trust or buy insurance to fund your funeral, it is wise to consider making a member of your family the beneficiary. If you make a mortician the beneficiary, you have committed your money to a particular funeral home. But your family might want to make a different choice if circumstances change.

VII. HOUSING: FINDING IT, KEEPING IT, AND MAINTAINING IT

This section addresses housing issues such as home ownership and programs intended to maintain the homes of seniors, including programs for both light maintenance and home repair provided by some cities and towns. It also addresses landlord-tenant issues, particularly the provisions of the Anti-Eviction Act directly relevant to seniors; condominium conversions and the particular statutory rights of seniors; and reverse mortgages for home owners with equity in their homes and a need for access to additional income. This section also considers housing alternatives such as senior housing, continuing care retirement communities, and supported living arrangements. The chapters in this section address the following questions:

- Can I get help with yard chores?
- Can I get assistance in paying my utility bills?
- Is there a way to get cash without having to sell and move out of my home?
- If I sell my house, will I have to pay taxes on the proceeds?
- My landlord wants to evict me, but I am ill. Can I prevent him from making me move?
- How do I get my security deposit returned to me?
- If my apartment building becomes a condominium and I do not want to buy, will I have to move?
- If I live in senior housing, can I keep a pet?
- Where can I get information about senior housing or retirement communities?
- What should I consider before I sign a contract to move into a continuing care retirement community?

17. Home Ownership

MAINTAINING YOUR PROPERTY

Minnie lives in a house in an urban neighborhood. The house is falling into poor condition, but she cannot afford to hire someone to fix it. She is most worried about the roof, which has begun to leak.

Minnie can get help from her community to help keep her house livable. She may be eligible for free or low-cost repair of the roof, which is her most crucial need, if her community provides such a program. She should contact the city or her county Office on Aging.

A number of programs are available to assist you with chores and home repair if you are having difficulty keeping up by yourself. The goal of these programs is to enable you to stay in your home even as you become less able to maintain the property. Most of these programs are staffed by volunteers, so it is difficult to know exactly what will be available in your community at any given time. But contact your county Office on Aging (see appendix A) to see what is offered in your area. You may need to be placed on a waiting list.

The county Offices on Aging provide chore services and fix-it or home maintenance programs. Chore services help with yard and lawn maintenance, snow clearing, light painting, and heavy house cleaning. In addition to services provided through your county Office on Aging, some schools and community groups provide help. Fix-it or home maintenance programs provide light repairs. You must pay for materials, but the Office on Aging will provide the labor.

You may be able to get assistance with financing more extensive repairs through a loan or grant program. The Farmer's Home Administration (FmHA) and Community Development Block Grants (CDBGs) provide funding to counties and municipalities with which to provide low-interest loans and/or grants for repairs and renovations. The New Jersey Department of Community Affairs, which has an office in each county, has a weatherization program that provides loans and grants to be used to improve insulation and reduce heating costs.

TAKING ADVANTAGE OF THE VALUE OF YOUR HOME

If you have owned your home for some time, you have built up equity that can be very valuable. Your investment in your home clearly pays off when you sell the home, but it can be useful to you while you continue to live there. Depending on your need for cash, you might want to consider one of the following approaches to tap into this equity without selling your house.

HOME EQUITY LOANS. A traditional home equity loan allows you to borrow against the equity in your house by placing a mortgage on the property. You receive cash or a line of credit in exchange for a security interest in your property. If you have an existing mortgage on the house, a home equity loan will be available for only a percentage of the value of your house that you already own. For example, if your house is worth $100,000 and you have a $60,000 mortgage balance, you have equity of $40,000. A lender will offer you a home equity loan for a percentage of your $40,000 equity. The lender will have a security interest, meaning that if you do not pay the balance due, the lender can use foreclosure proceedings to take your house.

You have the right to receive certain information before signing a home equity loan. The law requires that the lender make clear to you the amount of interest you will be paying, what it will take to pay off the loan in full, and whether there will be a large final payment required (known as a balloon payment). Make sure you understand what you are signing and what you are agreeing to do. A home equity loan can be an excellent source of cash, but it will put your house at risk if you have trouble paying the loan back. You should be sure you will be able to make the required payments and that you understand whether the payments will get higher over the life of the loan. If the loan has an adjustable interest rate, you should know how much the payments can change and how often this can happen.

REVERSE MORTGAGES

Marian has lived in the house she owns for thirty-eight years. She raised her family there, but has been living alone since her husband died seven years ago. Her income is limited; she receives Social Security benefits and a small pension from her husband's former employer. The house is paid for, but Marian is struggling to keep up with the taxes, and now she has received notice that the

Municipal Utilities Authority is putting a lien on her house for $16,500 for sewer work for which she has not paid. Marian is afraid that she will lose her home because she cannot pay this bill, but she does not want to move.

Marian may be a good candidate for a reverse mortgage. She has most of her assets tied up in a house that is fully paid for, and she wants to remain in her home. A reverse mortgage will pay her for the equity in her house. She can receive the funds in the form of a lump sum, as a monthly amount, or as a line of credit. She will be able to pay off the lien, will also receive additional monthly income, and will not have to pay back the mortgage until she leaves her house and it is sold or until her death. This will mean that she will not be able to leave the house to her children, but since her debts exceed her cash assets at this point, she needs more income in order to stay in the house.

UNDERSTANDING THE LAW. Reverse mortgages are designed to allow seniors to gain access to the equity built up in their homes without having to sell and move out of them. Your equity is the amount of money you would get if you sold your house. If you do not want to have to move, a reverse mortgage will allow you to get money for the house now. It is similar to a home equity loan, except that it does not have to be repaid until you choose to sell the house or until your death.

There are several types of reverse mortgages, but they all allow you to borrow money against the equity built up in your home. Repayment is not due until you leave the home permanently and it is sold to pay back the money borrowed. Reverse mortgages are available to those over the age of sixty-two who own their own homes. The amount available for you to borrow depends on your age, the value of your house, and current interest rates. The older you are and the higher the appraised value of your house, the more money will be available. The value of your house limits the amount that will have to be repaid. If your house is sold for an amount that does not cover the amount you received, the lender cannot pursue any of your other assets to get repaid.

If you are married, the lender will base its evaluation of your life expectancy on whichever of you is younger. This is because it is assumed that the younger spouse will remain in the house until his or her death. Since how much you will receive will be based, in part, on how long you are expected to remain in the home, the lender will determine this based on the life of whichever of you is expected to live longer.

The most widely available reverse mortgages are administered by the Federal Housing Administration (FHA) Reverse Mortgage Program. This program is also known as the Home Equity Conversion Mortgage (HECM) program. In order to be eligible for these federally insured reverse mortgages, you must meet the following criteria: you must be sixty-two or older, you must own and occupy a single-family one-unit home or an FHA-approved condominium, you must have little or no mortgage balance (any balance must be paid off), and you must maintain the home as your principal residence for the duration of the reverse mortgage.

If you are eligible, there are a variety of payment options available. You can select one of the following:

- Monthly payments for a predetermined number of months (a "term-fixed" mortgage).
- Monthly payments for as long as you live in the home (a "tenure-fixed" mortgage).
- Cash available as needed (a line of credit).

Before you decide on a reverse mortgage, carefully consider all of the implications of the agreement. No repayment will be required until the last living borrower dies, sells the home, or permanently moves away. Because there will be no monthly repayment, the amount you owe will grow larger with time. As the debt grows larger, the amount of cash you would have left after selling the house and paying off the loan will grow smaller. But you can never owe more than the value of the home. There may be other options available to you, so carefully consider whether a reverse mortgage is the right choice. For example, there may be programs that provide cash or services without requiring you to take a loan against your home.

The advantage of these loans is that they are guaranteed by the FHA, so that if the lender fails, you will continue to receive payments. The limitation is that the FHA puts a cap on how much you can receive; if the value of your house is below the limit, you should not be affected. In addition, the money you receive is not considered income, so it is not taxable and does not affect eligibility for income-tested programs like SSI or Medicaid. It might, however, affect your eligibility if it means you have assets over the permitted amount.

> ## FINDING A REVERSE MORTGAGE
>
> Contact a bank in your area and ask for information on federally guaranteed reverse mortgages. There are a number of programs in New Jersey. You can also get information from the American Association of Retired Persons (AARP) by calling (609) 987-0744.

There are alternatives to FHA reverse mortgages. These include reverse mortgages backed by private insurance and uninsured reverse mortgages. Without the guarantee of the Federal Housing Administration, make sure you understand what you are getting. If the loan relies on private insurance, check into the fiscal health of the insurance company. A reverse mortgage is an investment, and you should be as comfortable with the future soundness of the lender as you would be with any other investment. You are trading the equity in your house for the security of future income, so be sure you understand the terms and guarantees that will determine your financial future.

Other possible sources of funds include "sale-leasebacks" and deferred-payment loans. A sale-leaseback involves selling your house outright to an investor and then immediately renting it back under a long-term or lifetime lease. As the seller you will be financing the loan of the buyer, so you will receive monthly payments and still live in the house. But the money you receive will be viewed differently from that you would receive under a reverse mortgage, so it will have tax consequences. In addition, you will now be a tenant in your home, and you should be certain that it is clear who will pay for repairs, make tax payments, and pay for insurance.

Deferred-payment loans are sometimes available from government agencies in order to assist you with the maintenance of your home. The repayment of the loan will be secured by a lien on your property, but it will not have to be repaid until the house is sold. If you need money for maintenance purposes and such a program is available, this can be a relatively low-cost way to tap some of the equity of your home. But there will be more limitations on what you can do with the money than there will be if you choose another sources of funds. Contact your local government or County Office on Aging for more information.

KNOW WHAT YOU ARE AGREEING TO

If you receive a reverse mortgage, make sure you understand what you are agreeing to. A reverse mortgage is a loan, and you are agreeing to paying it back in the future from the sale of your house. You are committing the equity in your home to receive cash now, so it will not be available to you in the future or to your heirs after your death. You have the right, under the federal Truth-in-Lending Act, to receive detailed information about what you are paying. Make sure you receive expert advice before signing a reverse mortgage.

SELLING YOUR HOME AND PAYING TAXES ON IT

Until recently selling your house meant that you had to determine whether you were going to owe the federal government taxes for the gain you realized on the sale. Understanding that as people got older they might choose to move to smaller and less expensive homes, the federal government had allowed a one-time exclusion of gain from the sale of your principal residence. Since May of 1997, though, it has been even easier to avoid these taxes.

The law now provides that people who sell their principal residence can exclude up to $250,000 in gain from their gross income. This amount increases to $500,000 for a married couple filing jointly. This exclusion is available once every two years, so even if you took the one-time exclusion in the past you can still exclude the gain from your taxable income if you choose to sell your present house and move to a less expensive one.

GETTING HELP WITH PAYING YOUR BILLS

If your income is limited, you may be eligible to receive assistance that will cover some of your bills. Make sure you get all the benefits to which you are entitled. You may need to make some effort to get everything you should.

THE LIFELINE CREDIT PROGRAM. Lifeline Credit is a New Jersey program that will help you pay your utility bills if you are eligible. You can

---

WHERE TO GO FOR INFORMATION

For more information, write to Lifeline Credit, New Jersey Department of Health and Senior Services, CN-714, Trenton, NJ 08625-0714, or call (800) 792-9745. You may also call your county Office on Aging (see appendix A).

---

receive $225 credit on your utility bills per year if you meet the following requirements:

- You are at least sixty-five or you are receiving Social Security disability benefits.
- You have an annual income of less than $17,918 if you are single or less than $21,970 if you are married.
- You are a New Jersey resident.
- You or your spouse receives electric or gas bills in your name.

If you are enrolled in Pharmaceutical Assistance to the Aged and Disabled (PAAD) or any similar programs, you will automatically receive an application for Lifeline benefits (see chapter 3 for information about these programs). If you receive SSI benefits you already receive a supplement for the cost of utilities, so you will not be able to receive Lifeline benefits.

HELP WITH WATER AND SEWER BiLLS. Any city or county has the power to charge reduced rates or eliminate charges for water and sewer for those who meet the established guidelines. State law provides for these waivers if you are over sixty-five and disabled under the Social Security Administration regulations or rated over 60 percent disabled according to the Veterans Administration regulations. You must be eligible to receive assistance under the Pharmaceutical Assistance to the Aged and Disabled (PAAD) program or have a limited income. If you think you might be eligible for this type of assistance, contact your municipal or county water and sewer authority to determine whether it has such a program.

18. Tenant Issues

When you rent a place to live, you sign a contract in which you agree to pay the rent in exchange for housing and whatever services the landlord agrees to provide. The lease, which is the written agreement containing all the specifics of your contract, describes the rights and responsibilities of you as the tenant and of the landlord. But you both have legal obligations without regard to what the lease says. If you understand the law you will be able to enforce your rights as a tenant. You have some additional rights as a senior citizen. This section reviews common problems and addresses your rights in such situations.

PROTECTION FROM EVICTION

Grace rents her apartment, and her lease requires that she make a rent payment on the first day of each month. Grace's Social Security check, however, is not deposited into her bank account until the third day of the month. Even though she goes to the bank and gets a money order as soon as funds from the Social Security check are available, her landlord is always upset with her when she delivers her rent check after the first, and he has told her that she must pay on time. She does not have enough money from her small company pension to pay the rent until the funds from her Social Security check are available.

The landlord cannot force Grace to pay her rent until the fifth day of the month because she receives a government pension, Social Security. New Jersey law requires that any senior citizen who receives Social Security, a railroad retirement pension, or any other governmental pension in place of Social Security must be given five days' grace for payment when the rent is due on the first day of the month (N.J.S.A. 2A:42-6.1).

This law modifies the rule that is set forth in the lease. The lease establishes a day on which the rent is due. If it is late, the lease may require Grace to pay a late fee. But this law gives her the right to pay late without paying the late fee. It is important to note that if this law did not apply to Grace or if she were to pay after the fifth day of the month, she would have to pay a late fee. In addition, if she repeatedly pays late that will give the landlord the right to evict her, even if she always pays the late fee. The law says that except for the circumstances that excuse Grace from paying on the first of the month, the landlord should not have to wait for the rent to be paid. So do not make the mistake of thinking you are protected; regularly paying rent late is grounds for eviction.

> *Maria has lived in her apartment for eight years. Her daughter installed a small washing machine and dryer for her about four years ago when it became difficult for her to get to the laundry room in the basement with a load of laundry. Recently Maria received a notice from the landlord saying that she would have to get rid of the washer and dryer or move, since no tenant was permitted to have his or her own machines. Maria does not want to move, and she is very reluctant to ask her daughter to help her by doing laundry for her. She just wants to keep the washer and dryer.*

Maria may be entitled to keep the washer and dryer, but she may have to go to court to enforce her rights. The New Jersey Anti-Eviction Act (N.J.S.A. 2A:18–61 et seq.) gives her some rights, but not the right to violate reasonable rules of the lease. But the federal Fair Housing Act and its amendments (42 U.S.C.A. Sec. 3601 et seq.) may require her landlord to allow her to keep the washing machine and dryer, even if other tenants are not permitted to have their own machines.

LEGAL ISSUES. If you are a tenant, your contractual agreement with the landlord is governed by your lease. A lease can be written or oral. It should tell you the term of the lease and the rent that is due, but also list any rules and regulations you must follow; what late charges, if any, will be assessed; and how to renew or end your lease at the end of the term.

Landlord-tenant relationships are governed by the New Jersey Anti-Eviction Act. The statute lists the reasons for which a landlord can evict a tenant. These include not paying your rent, repeatedly paying your rent late (even if you pay the late fee), violating rules of the lease, and refusing to accept reasonable changes in the lease. Unless the landlord can prove to the court that one of the reasons listed in the statute exists, the landlord is not entitled to evict you, even at the end of the lease. The only exceptions to this are circumstances in which the statute does not apply, such as when the building has three or fewer apartments and the landlord lives in the building.

If your landlord tells you that you have to move out of your apartment or house and you do not want to move, get more information about this law to see if any of the provisions apply to you. Some of the provisions of this statute have been interpreted by the courts to provide additional protections to a tenant, so this is a case in which the plain meaning of the language of the statute may not decide the outcome of your case.

If you are terminally ill or suffer from some other hardship, the court has the power to delay your eviction for up to a year as long as you pay your rent. In addition, there are a number of specific requirements the landlord must meet before evicting you. If one of the requirements has not been met, such as giving you proper notice of what is wrong, the landlord must start the process over. But unless you point out what was not done properly, the court will not do it for you and the process will go ahead. You should seek legal help if you do not want to move. You might be entitled to prevent or at least delay your eviction.

The landlord must go to court to get an order to evict you. It is not legal for the landlord to try to force you out without a court order. Turning off utilities, locking you out of the apartment, or taking your property to force you to pay is illegal. Call the police if your landlord tries to take any of these steps.

It is important to note that your lease is renewable at the end of the term unless the landlord can prove one of the legal bases for ending your tenancy. The landlord can charge a higher rent (unless your home is covered by a rent-control law) or modify other terms of the lease at the end of the lease period. If you do not accept the new rent or terms, you can choose to move out instead of renewing. Follow the terms of your lease if you want to give your landlord notice that you are moving or, if the lease does not tell you what to do, give the landlord notice that you choose not to renew. Otherwise the landlord is entitled to assume that your lease will automatically be renewed.

In addition to the Anti-Eviction Act and related case law, there may be other laws that benefit you. Maria's story illustrates this kind of problem. The Anti-Eviction Act gives the landlord the right to enforce "reasonable" rules and to evict tenants who do not follow the rules. But

the federal Fair Housing Act and its amendments require nondis-
crimination in housing, even that owned by private citizens. This act
requires that a landlord make exceptions to or change rules that have
the effect of discriminating against a person with a disability. The
requirement of "reasonable accommodation," as it is termed in the
statute, makes it possible for Maria to argue that because her physical
condition makes it difficult or impossible for her to use the laundry
room as other tenants do, she should be able to keep her washing
machine and dryer. There are limits to what will be considered reasonable, however. The statute does not give tenants with disabilities the
right to do whatever they want without regard to the rules. But it does
require accommodation that is deemed reasonable.

PETS

Your landlord may not want you to keep a pet. The landlord is
generally permitted to restrict your right to have a pet unless you
live in senior housing or federally assisted housing. If your lease says
that no pets are allowed, in most cases a court will enforce that
provision and allow the landlord to evict you if you have a pet. The
exceptions to this rule are if you can prove that the landlord has
known about your pet and allowed it to stay, if other tenants have
pets and the landlord is not seeking to evict them, or if you had a pet
when the landlord took over the building.

If you live in rental housing that receives federal assistance, you
must be permitted to own and keep a pet. Your property receives
federal assistance if it is public housing or if it is privately owned but
the owner received or receives federal money to help with the building
or operation of the property. You are entitled to keep any pet that does
not cause a health or safety hazard, including a dog, cat, bird, or fish.
The landlord can place reasonable limits on the number of pets you
are allowed, but cannot prohibit pets altogether.

Your landlord can make rules about your pet that you must follow.
If you are permitted to keep a pet but you do not follow the rules, such
as keeping your pet on a leash or proving the pet has had required shots,
you can be evicted for violating the rules. If you do not follow the rules
you can be forced to either give the pet away or move out. The landlord
can also ask that you pay an additional security deposit for the pet, but
it can be no more than one month's rent. If you live in subsidized

housing you have the right to pay the additional security deposit over time until the full amount is deposited.

There is a similar state law that applies to apartment buildings for seniors with three or more units, including senior condominiums and cooperatives. These are housing developments for persons over age sixty-two (with spouses who are at least fifty-five). Again, the landlord can make rules about how a pet is kept and can require additional security, but you have the right to keep a pet. If your pet has offspring, the landlord can require you to give them away when they are eight weeks old.

SECURITY DEPOSITS

Joseph and Sarah live in a small apartment they moved into after their children left home. They have lived there for eight years, and over the years the building has become less and less pleasant. They do not like their neighbors, and some of the teenagers who hang out around the entrance make them nervous. They had been considering moving to a senior housing complex when new neighbors moved in next door. The new family was very noisy, sometimes keeping them up all night with loud parties. There were often people in the building's courtyard, and some of them may have been using drugs. When Joseph and Sarah complained, the building manager told them there was nothing she could do to help. Joseph and Sarah felt they had to move out, and as soon as they found a new apartment they told the building manager and moved within two weeks. After they moved out the landlord told them that they had broken the lease and would not receive their security deposit back.

If they cannot negotiate a resolution with the landlord, Joseph and Sarah have the right to go to small claims court to seek the return of their security deposit. New Jersey law provides that if a landlord wrongfully withholds the security deposit the tenant is entitled to receive double the amount that should have been returned. If Joseph and Sarah go to court, the judge will have to decide how much they should have received, and then will order the landlord to pay them twice that amount. If the tenants did not give adequate notice of their departure, the landlord may be entitled to keep a portion of the security deposit, but not the entire amount.

In general, you do not have the right to break your lease before the term of the lease has ended. If you move out without giving the landlord proper notice or without waiting until the end of the lease term, your landlord can keep your security deposit and can sue you for unpaid rent if the apartment is not rerented to a new tenant. But the law specifies some reasons for which you could move without waiting for the lease to end. Whether you meet these can be hard to determine without legal advice, so if you want to move during the term of your lease you should either contact your landlord and negotiate an agreement or consult an attorney about your right to move.

LEGAL ISSUES. If your landlord does not return your security deposit within thirty days after you move, you can file a complaint in small claims court. If the landlord wrongfully refused to return your deposit, the court must order the landlord to pay you double the amount of the wrongfully withheld deposit (N.J.S.A. 46:8-21.1). It is not expensive and quite easy to represent yourself, so if you think you can make a good claim that you should get your security deposit back, it is worth making this effort. Just call or go to the small claims court in your county and ask for a complaint form. Complete the form, stating what you want the court to do and why.

Joseph and Sarah from our story filed a small claims complaint that stated the following: "The defendant, our landlord, wrongfully withheld $415 from our security deposit after we moved. We were entitled to our full security deposit because the defendant failed to respond to unlivable conditions in the apartment we rented. We are now, therefore, entitled to double the amount wrongfully withheld plus costs and interest." The court will send your complaint to your landlord and set a court date. On the assigned day, you and the landlord will have to appear in court and try to settle the case by agreeing between the two of you. If you cannot agree, you will go in front of the judge and tell the judge what you think you should receive and why. Joseph and Sarah argued that they were constructively evicted—that is, forced to move because their apartment had become essentially unlivable and their landlord had failed to do anything to protect them. If the judge agrees with them, the landlord will be ordered to pay them their security deposit plus additional money for damages for initially refusing to return their security deposit.

LEARN MORE ABOUT YOUR RIGHTS

A booklet entitled *Tenants' Rights in New Jersey* is available for $5 from Legal Services of New Jersey, P.O. Box 1357, Edison, NJ 08818-1357.

UNDERSTANDING THE LAW. The most that your landlord can require as a security deposit is one and a half times your monthly rent. The landlord must deposit your security deposit in a separate interest-bearing bank account and provide you with written notice that this has been done. If the landlord does not follow this provision or the related requirements as to how to treat your security deposit, you are entitled to ask him to apply the security deposit toward your rent, and the landlord will then not have a security deposit for you. If you think that your landlord is not following these rules, check the statute and get more information about the law. Legal Services of New Jersey has information available that will help you to understand what your landlord must do with your security deposit.

Once you move out, the landlord must either return your deposit with interest or give you a complete list of damages he claims are your fault. You can be charged only for damages that are more than ordinary wear and tear. If the landlord claims that some or all of your deposit will not be returned because of damage to the apartment, you are entitled to an accounting of how much it will cost to repair the damage, and the landlord must return any extra money to you.

Normal wear and tear includes anything that could be expected to develop over time, such as worn carpets, faded wallpaper, peeling paint, or loose tiles. If appliances are not working, the issue will be whether they simply wore out, which would be considered normal wear and tear, or were rendered inoperable by misuse, which would not be considered normal wear and tear. If there is damage that is not thought to be due to normal wear and tear, you can be charged. For example, if something such as a window is broken or there are cigarette burns in carpeting or holes in the walls, you will be held responsible. By the way, if you leave your apartment clean, the landlord cannot charge you a cleaning fee.

If your landlord sells the property while you are living there, your security deposit plus interest must be turned over to the new owner.

ADVICE WHEN MOVING FROM AN APARTMENT

Before you return your key, ask the landlord or building manager to go through the apartment with you. Have him or her write down any damage or soil that will be charged to you. Get a signed statement so that there will not be any question later as to the condition the apartment was in when you left. If you cannot get the landlord or building manager to do this, ask a friend to do this with you, and take pictures of the apartment. Put a date on the pictures. If the landlord later claims there is damage that you do not think is your fault, the pictures will help you to argue that the apartment was in good condition when you left.

The new owner is responsible for obtaining your deposit when purchasing the property, and he or she must return it to you when you move following the rules discussed earlier. Even if the new owner never actually receives the money from the previous landlord, you are entitled to get your deposit back. The new owner cannot tell you to go to the previous owner to get your money back (N.J.S.A. 46:8-21).

GETTING HELP WITH PAYING YOUR BILLS

If your income is limited, you may be eligible to receive assistance that will cover some of your bills. Make sure you get all the benefits to which you are entitled. You may need to make some effort to get everything you should.

THE LIFELINE CREDIT PROGRAM. Lifeline Credit is a New Jersey program that will help you pay your utility bills if you are eligible. You can receive $225 credit on your utility bills per year if you meet the following requirements:

- You are at least sixty-five or you are receiving Social Security disability benefits.
- You have an annual income of less than $17,918 if you are single or less than $21,970 if you are married.
- You are a New Jersey resident.
- You or your spouse receives electric or gas bills in your name or the cost of utilities is included in your rent.

WHERE TO GO FOR INFORMATION

For more information, write to Lifeline Credit, New Jersey Department of Health and Senior Services, CN-714, Trenton, NJ 08625-0714, or call (800) 792-9745. You may also call your county Office on Aging (see Appendix A).

If you are enrolled in Pharmaceutical Assistance to the Aged and Disabled (PAAD) or any similar programs, you will automatically receive an application for Lifeline benefits (see chapter 3 for information about these programs). If you receive SSI benefits you already receive a supplement for the cost of utilities, so you will not be able to receive Lifeline benefits. If you qualify, you will receive a credit on your bills. If your utilities are included in your rent, you will receive a check.

HELP WITH WATER AND SEWER BILLS. Any city or county has the power to charge reduced rates or eliminate charges for water and sewer for those who meet the established guidelines. State law provides for these waivers if you are over sixty-five and disabled under the Social Security Administration regulations or rated over 60 percent disabled according to the Veterans Administration regulations. You must be eligible to receive assistance under the Pharmaceutical Assistance to the Aged and Disabled (PAAD) program or have a limited income. If you think you might be eligible for this type of assistance, contact your municipal or county water and sewer authority to determine whether it has such a program.

CONDOMINIUM CONVERSION

Gwen lives in an apartment in a large building. She has lived there since her husband died, and she finds it very convenient. She can walk to the grocery store and to the library, and there are some small stores nearby. There is a bus stop close to the building, so she can take the bus if she needs to go anywhere else. Her neighbors know her, and she feels safe in the building. Her rent is affordable with her pension and Social Security. But the building was recently purchased by a new owner, and Gwen does not know what is going to happen. She received a letter telling her that the building was going to be renovated and converted to condominiums. The letter said she would have the right to buy her apartment, but Gwen is not sure she wants to buy anything, and she is afraid she will have to move if she does not want to buy. She does not think she would be able to find another apartment she would like as much or that was as convenient.

If the building owner wants to convert the apartments in Gwen's building to condominiums, he or she must follow a number of rules. Gwen must be given the right to purchase her apartment before it is offered to anyone else. If she does not want to buy the apartment, she can ask the landlord to find her comparable housing. She may be entitled to one month's rent to cover moving expenses. In addition, if Gwen is sixty-two years old, her income is under $50,000 per year (or less than three times the county's average personal income if that is more), and she has lived in the building for at least one year, she is protected by the Senior Citizens and Disabled Protected Tenancy Act (N.J.S.A. 2A:18–61.24). This protection will allow her to stay in her apartment for up to forty years, even if the rest of the building becomes condominium units.

UNDERSTANDING THE LAW. When a rental building is converted to condominiums, the law provides a number of protections for tenants. The most important thing to remember is that your landlord cannot evict you in order to sell your apartment without following the exact requirements of the law. Even if the landlord follows every requirement, you should have at least three years before you must move out. You can get assistance from the landlord with finding a new apartment and covering moving expenses.

If you ask your landlord to help you find comparable housing to move into, you can expect to be shown housing that is similar to where you already live. The apartment must be similar in terms of size, number of bedrooms, and any special accessibility features. It should also be equal to where you live in terms of access to the community and to public transportation. If you send your landlord specific reasonable requests in writing regarding the criteria you are looking for in a new place to live, he should try to honor them. If the landlord does not assist you with finding comparable housing, you are entitled to more time before you can be forced to move.

If you are entitled to a protected tenancy under the Senior Citizens and Disabled Protected Tenancy Act, you have an even greater right to protection from eviction. You will have to complete an application to establish that you are entitled to this protection. Once you are found to have a protected tenancy, you can expect to be able to stay in your apartment for forty years if you wish. You will still have to pay the rent and follow the rules and regulations of the building; if the landlord has another valid reason to evict you, the law will not protect you. But if you pay your rent and follow the rules, you will be protected from having your apartment sold as a condominium. The landlord also cannot raise your rent in order to pay the cost of the conversion, although reasonable rent increases are allowed. The landlord is permitted to raise the rent if you receive more services after the conversion. If your rent is going up and you live in a town with a rent control law, you can contact the Rent Control Board. If you are concerned about whether your landlord is following these rules, you should contact an attorney.

19. Alternative Housing Arrangements

FINDING NEW LIVING ARRANGEMENTS

When you want or need to find new housing, consider one of the various options available to seniors in New Jersey. This chapter describes the various types of housing catering to the needs of seniors, and it provides information about locating different housing options. The growing numbers of people of retirement age in the state has meant a growth in options available to you. There is a range of types of housing offering various services depending on your physical needs and the resources you have available.

Whatever choice you make about new housing, make sure you understand what is offered and what promises are being made for the future. If you are expecting medical or nursing home care, if needed, within the community you join, consider that you are essentially buying insurance and think about whether you will get your money's worth. The next section of this chapter describes the range of different senior housing options available. The following section considers issues to which you should pay attention when deciding what move is best for you.

HOUSING OPTIONS

There are many different types of senior housing. Before you make a decision about which is right for you, consider what makes them different. Some offer the option to rent your residence; others require that you buy. Some are exclusively or primarily residences; some provide a range of services. If services are provided, do you pay a flat rate for necessary services, or do you pay for each service as it is used? The range of services also varies, from arranging social and recreational activities to providing full nursing care. Consider not only your requirements at the time you move, but what you are likely to need or want in the future.

ADULT RETIREMENT COMMUNITIES. Adult retirement communities are communities designed for independent older people who are not in need of intensive medical services. Most retirement communities are made up of units you purchase, but some rentals are available. The units can be single-family houses, duplexes, condominiums, or garden apartments. Adult retirement communities generally offer social and recreational activities such as swimming, tennis, and golf; a clubhouse; and some other services, such as transportation for shopping. No medical or nursing services are regularly available, but communities can and sometimes do arrange for these services to be provided to residents.

A manager is responsible for the upkeep and general maintenance of the community, and a monthly fee is charged for these services. As a property owner, the resident is responsible for paying property taxes. The usual entrance age is fifty-five or older. These facilities are registered with the New Jersey Department of Community Affairs and the Office of Planned Real Estate Development.

ASSISTED LIVING RESIDENCES. Assisted living residences provide more intensive services than retirement communities. They are licensed by the Department of Health and Senior Services. They provide apartment-style housing and group dining to ensure that assisted living services are available when needed. Apartment units offer at least one unfurnished room, a private bathroom, a kitchenette, and a lockable door on the unit entrance. The design is intended to allow you as much independence and privacy as possible, with services available as needed. Assisted living services are coordinated to offer an array of supportive personal and health services that are available twenty-four hours a day to residents who have been assessed to need these services. This includes residents who require formal long-term care (nursing home care).

CONTINUING CARE RETIREMENT COMMUNITIES. A continuing care retirement community (CCRC) provides housing, services, and health care, including nursing home care, to people of retirement age. The community must provide a continuum of care to meet the needs of individual residents, beginning with independent living and continuing through skilled nursing care. The concept is that a person contracts with the community to provide different levels of care and service as his or her needs change. A CCRC offers a contract that is signed when the person first enters the community. The contract will define the type of housing and services to be provided. Meals, housekeeping, linens, twenty-four–hour security, and recreational services are usually provided.

Generally there is a substantial entrance fee (ranging from $40,000 to over $200,000) that guarantees shelter and access to various health care services, whether these services are prepaid or provided on a fee-for-service basis. Monthly fees are also charged. CCRCs are regulated by the New Jersey Department of Community Affairs, CCRC Section. Consumers who wish to receive a guide for selecting a CCRC may call the New Jersey Department of Community Affairs at (609) 530-5448.

MULTILEVEL FACILITIES. Multilevel facilities offer a number of residences that provide two or more levels of service. These levels range from independent living to different types of supportive services to skilled nursing care. Multilevel facilities usually do not offer contract agreements pertaining to moving from one level to another, nor do they charge a substantial entrance fee. However, priority to move from one level to another is usually given to residents already living in some part of the development.

RESIDENTIAL HEALTH CARE FACILITIES. Residential health care facilities provide health maintenance and monitoring services under the direction of a professional nurse. They provide each person with a room, meals, linens, housekeeping, personal assistance, personal laundry, twenty-four–hour security, financial management, recreation, supervision of medication, and limited health services. A room and bath may be private or shared. Most services are included in the rent, but some may be purchased separately. These facilities are licensed by the New Jersey Department of Health and Senior Services.

MOBILE HOME PARKS. Mobile home parks have spaces where manufactured housing units may be located and hooked up to utilities such as water, electricity, and heat. Generally you purchase your own unit and rent the space from the mobile home park. A mobile home park can be restricted to people who are fifty-five years of age or older. Because you own the unit but rent the land where your unit rests, the New Jersey landlord-tenant law governs your relationship with the park owner. You should understand what the landlord is obliged to provide and what is your responsibility. Since most units are not designed to be moved once they are put into place, you may have some restrictions on your ability to sell the unit if the contract with the park owner requires approval prior to a sale.

SUBSIDIZED APARTMENTS FOR THE ELDERLY. Subsidized apartments for the elderly are rental units, generally in the form of garden apartments or high-rise or low-rise buildings. The units have been specially designed for and limited to people who are over sixty-two years old or disabled. There are income limitations for eligibility for this type of housing, and the rents are often subsidized, with the amount of rent based on your household income. There are often lengthy waiting lists for this type of housing. In some types of subsidized housing, recreational activities and support services such as meals, housekeeping, or transportation are provided. Fees for services may be included in the rent or charged separately. For information, contact the Housing Authority in the county or municipality where you would like to live.

BOARDING HOMES. There are a number of boarding homes for older adults in New Jersey. Class A homes provide only rooms and baths, but no other services. Class B and Class C homes provide rooms, baths, linens, and meals. In addition, Class C homes provide twenty-four-hour supervision and personal and financial services, including the monitoring of self-administered medications. Other services may also be provided, such as transportation to medical appointments. All homes are licensed by the New Jersey Department of Community Affairs and the Bureau of Rooming and Boarding House Standards.

SHARED LIVING RESIDENCES. Shared living residences are homes in which unrelated persons live together. A residence may be owned cooperatively, sponsored by a nonprofit organization, or owned or managed by a person who continues to reside there. Each person has a private room. Bathrooms are either private or shared. All other spaces in the house are shared. A group residence usually accommodates between five and fifteen people who furnish and clean their own rooms. A volunteer or paid manager is responsible for overall maintenance, housekeeping, shopping, and dinner preparation. Breakfast and lunch may be prepared individually. Most group residences are licensed as Class B or Class C boarding homes.

NURSING HOMES OR LONG-TERM CARE FACILITIES. These facilities are designed for patients who need twenty-four-hour nursing supervision, many of whom are confined to bed for some portion of the day or who are incontinent. These facilities offer medical treatment under the supervision of licensed nurses, and at least one registered nurse must be on duty during the day. Long-term care facilities are licensed by the New Jersey Department of Health.

MAKING HOUSING DECISIONS

Depending on the type of housing you choose, you will probably have to sign either a rental agreement or a contract. Make sure you understand what is covered in any document you sign, especially if you are contracting for services you expect to use in the future. Whether it is the preparation of meals in a shared residence or the provision of nursing care in a continuing care community, your contract will define your expectations for the future. If something is not written into the agreement, you will not be able to force the management to provide it if circumstances change. If you do not understand something in the agreement, ask questions.

Some particular issues to consider are as follows:

- What do you know about the financial soundness of the community? If you are purchasing an interest in a community, you want to know that your investment is sound. Even more important, you are planning to live in the community, and you want to be assured that the services you need will be in place when you need them. Think ahead, and investigate whether the management is reliable. Seek expert advice, just as you would if you were buying a house or insurance.
- Do you understand the fee structure of the community? Make sure you know what is included and what will require additional fees. Also consider whether fees will remain stable. Find out what increases there have been in the past in order to gauge what you can expect.
- Does the agreement allow you to change your mind? Make sure you understand what fees are refundable if you do change your mind.
- If you are considering a community with different levels of care available, do you understand what process will be followed in determining a move? You will want to have some control over when you move into nursing home care, and you should understand what your rights will be. Similarly, find out what right you

have to maintain your apartment if you are hospitalized or what rights one spouse has if the other requires a higher level of care.

GETTING INFORMATION ON FACILITIES AVAILABLE

There are a number of resources available to help you investigate your housing choices. This section helps you to locate facilities in New Jersey. Make sure you compare several facilities of whatever type you consider so that you will fully understand the range of choices possible.

SENIOR HOUSING LISTS. The New Jersey Division of Senior Affairs maintains lists of the following types of senior housing:

- Continuing care retirement communities;
- Adult retirement communities;
- Government subsidized housing;
- Shared housing;
- House-matching programs.

For copies of these lists, write the New Jersey Division of Senior Affairs at CN-807, Trenton, New Jersey 08625-0807, or call (800) 792-8820.

ADULT COMMUNITY REGULATIONS. Information on the regulations that apply to adult retirement communities and continuing care communities is available from the Division of Codes and Standards of the New Jersey Department of Community and Urban Affairs at CN-805, Trenton, NJ 08625-0805, or you may call (609) 530-5474 for adult retirement communities or (609) 530-5448 for continuing care retirement communities.

THE CONGREGATE HOUSING SERVICES PROGRAM. The New Jersey Division of Senior Affairs contracts with a number of subsidized housing projects around the state to provide supportive environments to certain frail elderly persons with low income through its Congregate Housing Services Program. The cost to participants is on a sliding scale, based on income. For information, write to the Division of Senior Affairs, New Jersey Department of Health and Senior Services, at CN-807, Trenton, NJ 08625-0807, or call (800) 792-8820.

THE ASSISTED LIVING FACILITIES ASSOCIATION. The Assisted Living Facilities Association provides information about assisted living as an alternative to nursing home care, and a list of affiliated centers throughout the country. Call (703) 691-8100.

Appendix A. County Offices on Aging

Atlantic County

Office on Aging
201 Shore Road
Northfield, NJ 08225
(888) 426-9243

Bergen County

Department of Human Services
Administrative Building
Court Plaza South, 21 Main Street
Room 109W
Hackensack, NJ 07601-7000
(201) 646-2625

Burlington County

Office on Aging
49 Rancocas Road
P.O. Box 6000
Mount Holly, NJ 08060
(609) 265-5069

Camden County

Senior Services
The Parkview on the Terrace
700 Browning Road
Suite 11
West Collingswood, NJ 08107
(856) 858-3220

Cape May County

Department of Aging
Social Services Building
3509 Route 9, South

Rio Grande, NJ 08242
(609) 886-2784

Cumberland County

Office on Aging
590 Shallow Pike
Bridgeton, NJ 08302
(856) 453-8066

Essex County

Division on Aging
15 South Munn Avenue
Second Floor
East Orange, NJ 07018
(973) 678-9700

Gloucester County

Department on Aging
Route 45 and Budd Boulevard
P.O. Box 337
Woodbury, NJ 08096
(856) 384-6910

Hudson County

Office on Aging
595 County Avenue
Building 2
Secaucus, NJ 07094
(201) 271-4322

Hunterdon County

Office on Aging
Community Services Building
6 Gauntt Place
Flemington, NJ 08822-4614
(908) 788-1363

Mercer County

Office on Aging
640 South Broad Street
Trenton, NJ 08650
(609) 989-6661

Middlesex County

Office on Aging
841 Georges Road
North Brunswick, NJ 08902
(732) 745-3293

Monmouth County

Office on Aging
Hall of Records Annex
One East Main Street
Freehold, NJ 07728-1255
(732) 431-7450

Morris County

Department of Human Services
Division on Aging
30 Schuyler Place
Third Floor
P.O. Box 900
Morristown, NJ 07963-0900
(800) 564-4656

Ocean County

Office of Senior Services
First Floor, Building 2
1027 Hooper Avenue
P.O. Box 2191
Toms River, NJ 08754-2191
(800) 668-4899

Passaic County

Office on Aging
675 Goffle Road
Hawthorne, NJ 07506
(800) 223-0556

Salem County

Office on Aging
98 Market Street
Salem, NJ 08079
(856) 935-7510

Somerset County

Office on Aging
Information and Referral
P.O. Box 3000
County Administration Building
Somerville, NJ 08876
(908) 704-6346

Sussex County

Office on Aging
Department of Health and Senior Services
Division of the Office on Aging
12 Cork Hill Road
Franklin Senior Center
Franklin, NJ 07416
(973) 579-0555

Union County

Department of Human Services
Division on Aging
Union County Administration Building
Elizabethtown Plaza
Elizabeth, NJ 07207
(888) 280-8226

Warren County

Office on Aging
Wayne Dumont Jr. Administration Building
Suite 245
166 County Route 519 South
Belvidere, NJ 07823-1949
(908) 475-6591

Appendix B. Finding Legal Help

COUNTY LEGAL SERVICES OFFICES

Atlantic County Cape-Atlantic Legal Services

1261 Route 9 South
Cape May Court House, NJ 08210
(609) 465-3001

Provides free legal services to low-income clients in civil cases; advises on landlord-tenant issues, consumer bankruptcy, and entitlement appeals.

Bergen County Legal Services

47 Essex Street
Hackensack, NJ 07601
(201) 487-2166

Provides free legal services to low-income clients in civil cases; advises on all legal problems, and represents clients before all courts and administrative agencies.

Bergen County Legal Services to the Elderly Law Program

Legal Services to the Elderly
27 Warren Street
Suite 303
Hackensack, NJ 07601
(201) 487-2169

Provides a no-fee legal services program for senior citizens sixty and older without regard to income. Also provides information on legal rights and entitlements, legal counseling, and referrals to lawyers.

Burlington County Senior Citizen Lawyer Referral Program

Office on Aging
Human Services Facility
795 Woodlane Road

P.O. Box 6000
Westampton, NJ 08060
(609) 265-5069

Provides legal assistance to Burlington County residents sixty and older. Preference for service is given to those individuals with the greatest social and economic need.

Camden Regional Legal Services, Inc.

745 Market Street
Camden, NJ 08102-1117
(856) 964-2010

Provides free legal services to low-income clients in civil cases; advises on landlord-tenant issues, consumer fraud, entitlement appeals, and wills.

Cape May County Cape-Atlantic Legal Services

1261 Route 9, South
Cape May Court House, NJ 08210
(609) 465-3001

Provides free legal services to low-income clients in civil cases; advises on landlord-tenant issues, consumer bankruptcy, and entitlement appeals.

Cumberland County Free Wills Program

Cumberland County Surrogate's Office
Room 18 Court House
Bridgeton, NJ 08302
(856) 451-8000, ext. 219

Provides free wills to Cumberland County residents sixty and older. These are simple "no-frills" wills and do not include trusts and guardianships.

Cumberland County Senior Advocate Center

22 East Washington Street
Bridgeton, NJ 08302
(856) 451-0003

Provides free legal services for eligible persons sixty and older. Also provides home visits for the homebound.

Essex-Newark Legal Services

106 Halsey Street
Newark, NJ 07102
(973) 624-4500

Gloucester County Legal Assistance

(856) 848-5360

Gloucester County Wills for Seniors

P.O. Box 177
Woodbury, NJ 08096
(856) 853-3282

Provides free wills and living wills.

Hudson County Legal Services

574 Newark Avenue
Jersey City, NJ 07306
(201) 792-6363

Provides free legal services in civil matters to eligible individuals who are unable to retain a private attorney. Legal assistance and representation are provided on housing, consumer, and public entitlement issues.

Hunterdon County Legal Services

82 Park Avenue
Flemington, NJ 08822
(908) 782-7979

Provides free legal services in civil matters to eligible individuals who are unable to retain a private attorney. Legal assistance and representation are provided on housing, consumer, family law, and public entitlement issues.

Mercer County Legal Services Project for the Elderly

198 West State Street
Trenton, NJ 08618
(609) 695-6249

Provides free legal services in civil matters to eligible individuals sixty and older. Services include assistance with bankruptcy, foreclosure, landlord-tenant, family law, and public entitlement issues.

Middlesex County Legal Services Corporation

78 New Street, Third Floor
New Brunswick, NJ 08901
(732) 249-7600
    or
313 State Street, Suite 308
Perth Amboy, NJ 08861
(732) 324-1613

Provides free legal services in civil matters to eligible individuals who are unable to retain a private attorney. Legal assistance and representation are provided on landlord-tenant, public assistance, social security, food stamps, matrimonial, and family affairs issues.

Monmouth County Legal Services, Inc.

25 Broad Street
Freehold, NJ 07728
(732) 866-0020

Provides legal services to seniors, including advice on living wills and guardianships.

Morris County Legal Aid Society

30 Schuyler Place
P.O. Box 900
Morristown, NJ 07963-0900
(973) 285-6911

Provides advice on all aspects of legal matters for senior citizens. These services attempt to avoid costly court fees and ensure the legal rights of older persons.

Ocean/Monmouth County Legal Services

9 Robbins Street, Ste 2A
Toms River, NJ 08753
(732) 341-2727

Provides civil legal assistance to eligible low-income persons in Ocean and Monmouth Counties.

Ocean County Legal Services (Under the Older Americans Act)

P.O. Box 2191
Toms River, NJ 08754
(732) 929-2091

Provides limited legal services under the Older Americans Act by or under the supervision of an attorney to protect and secure the rights of older persons.

Passaic County Legal Aid Society

140 Market Street
Paterson, NJ 07505
(973) 345-7171

Provides paraprofessional legal services to senior citizens.

Salem County Legal Services

22 Washington Street
Bridgeton, NJ 08302
(856) 451-0003

Handles cases involving governmental benefits and entitlements, landlord-tenant relationships, protective services, and pensions at no cost to customers.

Somerset/Sussex County Legal Services

P.O. Box 159
Newton, NJ 07860
(973) 383-7400

Provides legal assistance on issues including welfare, Social Security, utility problems, and shutoffs for seniors sixty and older based on eligibility.

Union County Legal Aid

Union County Courthouse
New Annex, Room 307
Elizabeth, NJ 07207
(908) 527-4769

Provides services Wednesdays only, noon to 3:00 p.m.

Union County Legal Services Corporation

60 Prince Street
Elizabeth, NJ 07208
(908) 354-4340

Provides free legal help for those who are indigent on civil matters.

Warren County Legal Services for Senior Citizens

91 Front Street
P.O. Box 65
Belvidere, NJ 07823
(908) 475-3052

Provides free legal services in civil matters to eligible individuals who are unable to retain a private attorney. Provides legal assistance and representation on housing, consumer, family law, and public entitlement issues.

LEGAL REFERRAL SERVICES

Atlantic County Bar Association Lawyer Referral Service

1201 Bacharach Boulevard
Atlantic City, NJ 08401
(609) 345-3444

Bergen County Bar Association, Inc., Lawyers Referral Plan

61 Hudson Street
Hackensack, NJ 07601
(201) 488-0044

Burlington County Bar Association Lawyer Referral Service

117 High Street
Mount Holly, NJ 08060
(609) 261-4862

Camden County Bar Association Lawyer Referral Service

800 Hudson Square, Suite 103
P.O. Box 1027
Camden, NJ 08101
(856) 964-4520

Cape May County Bar Association Lawyer Referral Service

P.O. Box 425
Cape May Court House, NJ 08210
(609) 463-0313

Cumberland County Bar Association Lawyer Referral Service

P.O. Box 2031
Vineland, NJ 08360
(856) 692-6207

Essex County Bar Association Lawyer Referral Service

One Newark Center
Sixteenth Floor
Newark, NJ 07102-5268
(973) 622-6207

Gloucester County Bar Association Lawyer Referral Service

Justice Complex
P.O. Box 338
Woodbury, NJ 08096
(856) 848-4589

Hudson County Bar Association Lawyer Referral Service

583 Newark Avenue
Jersey City, NJ 07306
(201) 798-2727

Hunterdon County Bar Association Lawyer Referral Service

P.O. Box 267
Pittstown, NJ 08867
(908) 735-2611

Mercer County Bar Association Lawyer Referral Service

1245 Whitehorse-Mercerville Road
Suite 420
Mercerville, NJ 08619-3894
(609) 585-6200

Middlesex County Bar Association Lawyer Referral Service

87 Bayard Street
New Brunswick, NJ 08901
(732) 828-0053

Monmouth County Bar Association Lawyer Referral Service

Court House
Freehold, NJ 07728
(732) 431-5544

Morris County Bar Association Lawyer Referral Service

10 Park Place
Morristown, NJ 07960
(973) 267-5882

Ocean County Bar Association Lawyer Referral Service

Courthouse
P.O. Box 381
Toms River, NJ 08753
(732) 240-3666

Passaic County Bar Association Lawyer Referral Service

Court House
Hamilton Street
Paterson, NJ 07505
(973) 278-9223

Salem County Bar Association Lawyer Referral Service

(856) 935-5629

Somerset County Bar Association Lawyer Referral Service

P.O. Box 1095
Somerville, NJ 08876
(908) 685-2323

Sussex County Bar Association Lawyer Referral Service

10 Park Place
Morristown, NJ 07960
(973) 267-5882

Union County Bar Association Lawyer Referral Service

Courthouse
Third Floor
Elizabeth, NJ 07207
(908) 353-4715

Warren County Bar Association Lawyer Referral Service

10 Park Place
Morristown, NJ 07960
(973) 267-5882

COMMUNITY HEALTH LAW PROJECT

Bergen County Community Mental Health Law Project

327 Ridgewood Avenue
Paramus, NJ 07652-4895
(201) 599-6193

Camden County Community Health Law Project

900 Haddon Avenue
Suite 400
Collingswood, NJ 08108
(856) 858-9500

Provides free legal help for those with mental and physical disabilities on public entitlements, housing, landlord-tenant issues, and consumer fraud.

Essex County Community Health Law Project

185 Valley Street
South Orange, NJ 07079
(973) 275-1175
    or
650 Bloomfield Avenue
Second Floor
Bloomfield, NJ 07003
(973) 680-5599

Provides free legal help for those with mental and physical disabilities on public entitlements, housing, landlord-tenant issues, and consumer fraud.

Mercer County Community Health Law Project

114 West Lafayette Street
Trenton, NJ 08608
(609) 392-5553

Provides free legal help for those with mental and physical disabilities on public entitlements, housing, landlord-tenant issues, and consumer fraud.

Union County Community Health Law Project

65 Jefferson Avenue
Elizabeth, NJ 07201
(908) 355-8282

Provides free legal help for those with mental and physical disabilities on public entitlements and housing.

Appendix C. Social Security Administration Offices

Social Security Administration
6401 Security Boulevard
Baltimore, MD 21235
(410) 965-1234

Administers a national plan of contributory social insurance for people who are retired, deceased, or disabled and their dependents under 5 U.S.C. App. Reorganization Plan No. 1 of 1953.

Regional Office

40-102 Federal Building
26 Federal Plaza
New York, NY 10278
(212) 264-3915

Tele-Service Centers

Call for answers to questions and to set up appointments at branch or district offices.

754 Route 18
Second Floor
East Brunswick, NJ 08816
(800) 772-1213

2 Journal Square
Ninth Floor
Jersey City, NJ 07306
(800) 772-1213

District and Branch Offices

Visit the office most convenient for you. Claims representatives can assist you with applications and can help resolve problems.

317 Brick Boulevard
Brick, NJ 08723

149 West Broad Street
Bridgeton, NJ 08302

2600 Mount Ephriam Avenue
Camden, NJ 08104

68 South Harrison Street
East Orange, NJ 07018

Expressway Corporate Center
Suite III
100 Decadon Drive
Egg Harbor Township, NJ 08234

24-52 Rahway Avenue
Elizabeth, NJ 07202

51 Charles III Drive
Glassboro, NJ 08028

201 Rock Road
Suite 206
Glen Rock, NJ 07452-1740

22 Sussex Street
Hackensack, NJ 07601

5 Marineview Plaza
Hoboken, NJ 07030

686 Nye Avenue
Irvington, NJ 07111

190 Middlesex Turnpike
Iselin, NJ 08830-2842

861 Bergen Avenue
Jersey City, NJ 07306

396 Bloomfield Avenue
Montclair, NJ 07042

Lumberton Plaza
1636-19 Route 38
Mount Holly, NJ 08060

645 Neptune Boulevard
Neptune, NJ 07753

52 Charles Street
New Brunswick, NJ 08901

193 Avon Avenue
Newark, NJ 07108

970 Broad Street
Room 1035
Newark, NJ 07102

Sussex County Mall
15 Route 206 North
Newton, NJ 07860

1719 B, Route 10
Room 208
Parsippany, NJ 07054-4507

30 River Drive
Passaic, NJ 07055

21 Clark Street
Second Floor
Paterson, NJ 07505
  Mailing address:
    200 Federal Plaza
    Paterson, NJ 07505-1956

1700 West Front Street
Plainfield, NJ 07063-1022

Granetz Plaza
U.S. Highway 206 South
Raritan, NJ 08869

Rio Grande Plaza
Suite 7
1500 Wildwood Boulevard
Rio Grande, NJ 09242

8 Robbins Street
Toms River, NJ 08753

50 East State Street
Suite 228
Trenton, NJ 08608

Appendix D. County Surrogate Offices

Atlantic County

5911 Main Street
Mays Landing, NJ 08330
(609) 645-5800; fax (609) 645-5805
    or
1201 Bacharach Boulevard
Atlantic City, NJ 08401
(609) 343-2341

Bergen County

Justice Center
Room 211
10 Main Street
Hackensack, NJ 07601-7000
(201) 646-2252; Records Room (201) 646-2261

Burlington County

Court Complex
First Floor
49 Rancocas Road
Mount Holly, NJ 08060
(609) 265-5005

Camden County

Hall of Justice
Suite 609
101 South Fifth Street
Camden, NJ 08103-4001
(856) 225-7275

Cape May County

Courthouse Building
9 North Main Street
Cape May Court House, NJ 08210

Mailing address:
4 Moore Road
Cape May Court House, NJ 08210
(609) 463-6666; fax (609) 463-6454

Cumberland County

Court House
60 West Broad Street
Bridgeton, NJ 08302
(856) 453-4801; fax (856) 451-7356

Essex County

207 Hall of Records
465 Dr. Martin Luther King, Jr. Blvd.
Newark, NJ 07102
(973) 621-4900 or 621-4901 or 621-4902

Gloucester County

Surrogate's Building
First Floor
North Broad Street
P.O. Box 177
Woodbury, NJ 08096-7177
(856) 853-3282; fax (856) 853-3311

Hudson County

107 Administrative Building
595 Newark Avenue
Jersey City, NJ 07306
(201) 795-6377

Hunterdon County

Hunterdon County Justice Center
Park Avenue
Flemington, NJ 08822
(908) 788-1156

Mercer County

310 Courthouse Annex
209 South Broad Street
P.O. Box 8068
Trenton, NJ 08650-0068
(609) 989-6326

Middlesex County

Administrative Building
Seventh Floor
1 John F. Kennedy Square
New Brunswick, NJ 08901
(732) 745-3055; fax (732) 745-4125

Monmouth County

Hall of Records
1 East Main Street
Freehold, NJ 07728-1265
(732) 431-7330

Morris County

Administrative and Records Building
P.O. Box 900
Morristown, NJ 07963-0900
(973) 285-6500; fax (973) 829-8599

Ocean County

211 Courthouse
118 Washington Street
P.O. Box 2191
Toms River, NJ 08754
(732) 929-2011

Passaic County

77 Hamilton Street
Paterson, NJ 07505-2018
(973) 881-4760

Salem County

92 Market Street
Salem, NJ 08079-9856
(856) 935-7510, ext. 325; fax (856) 935-8882

Somerset County

20 Grove Street
P.O. Box 3000
Somerville, NJ 08876-1262
(908) 231-7003; fax (908) 429-8765

Sussex County

4 Park Place
Newton, NJ 07860-1795
(973) 579-0920; fax (973) 579-0909

Union County

Courthouse
Second Floor
2 Broad Street
Elizabeth, NJ 07207-6001
(908) 527-4280; fax (908) 351-9212

Warren County

413 Second Street
Belvidere, NJ 07823-1500
(908) 475-6223; fax (908) 475-6319

Appendix E. Victim Assistance

Atlantic County

Adult Protective Services (APS)
(609) 345-6700

Bergen County

APS-County Board of Social Services
(201) 368-4300

Burlington County

APS-County Welfare Board
(609) 261-1000

Camden County

APS-County Board of Senior Services
(856) 225-8138

Cape May County

APS-County Welfare Board
(609) 886-6200

Cumberland County

APS-County Guidance Center
(856) 825-6810

Essex County

APS-Community Health Law Project
(973) 672-0671

Gloucester County

APS-County Board of Social Services
(856) 582-9200

Hudson County

APS-County Board of Protective Services
(201) 295-5160

Hunterdon County

APS-County Board of Social Services
(908) 788-1300

Mercer County

APS-County Board of Social Services
(609) 989-4346

Middlesex County

APS-County Board of Social Services
(732) 745-3635

Monmouth County

APS-County Protective Services for the Elderly and Disabled
(732) 531-9191

Morris County

APS-County Board of Social Services
(973) 356-7282

Ocean County

APS-County Board of Social Services
(732) 349-1500

Passaic County

APS-County Board of Social Services
(973) 881-2600

Salem County

APS
(856) 935-7510 or (856) 358-3857

Somerset County

APS-County Board of Social Services
(908) 418-3400

Sussex County

APS-County Welfare Board
(973) 383-3600

Union County

APS-County Catholic Community Services
(908) 355-4949

Warren County

APS-County Welfare Board
(908) 475-4744

Appendix F. Glossary

activities of daily living (ADL) personal care activities, such as bathing, eating, dressing, and moving from bed to chair.

actuary a person who determines insurance rates using statistical calculations of risk.

adjustable-rate loan a secured loan without a fixed interest rate. Rates are tied to a specific interest figure and can fluctuate periodically, as provided for in loan documents. Adjustable-rate loans should include maximum and minimum rates and limits on the extent of change on any one change date.

administrator a person appointed to administer an estate when someone dies without a will.

adult day care facility a facility that provides services to adults with chronic conditions such as Alzheimer's disease. These services can include nursing and social activities.

advance directive a document intended to provide direction to family members and doctors regarding medical decision making.

alimony money paid under court order by a former spouse for support following or pending divorce proceedings.

annuity income paid at regular intervals for a fixed period, often the recipient's lifetime.

assisted living facility a housing arrangement that offers services for seniors such as medical supervision, meals, and social services.

assisted suicide suicide achieved with the help of another. A doctor might help to obtain a lethal dose of medication or provide assistance with the physical administration of medication.

attorney in fact the person named to act for the maker of a power of attorney.

autonomy independence or the ability to act for oneself.

balloon payment a single large final payment on a loan that otherwise required relatively low monthly payments.

beneficiary the recipient of a benefit or the recipient of an insurance payment or of property under a will.

bona fide occupational qualification (BFOQ) a hiring requirement that is necessary for the hiree to accomplish the job's tasks. A particular skill is usually a valid qualification, whereas race, gender, and age generally are not valid job requirements. In order to require job holders to be under a certain age, for example, an employer must show that being young is a valid requirement that is necessary for an employee to do the job itself.

COBRA benefits insurance continuation benefits required by the Consolidated Omnibus Reconciliation Act of 1985. These benefits allow individuals to purchase insurance at a group rate for eighteen months after the termination of employment.

codicil a change added to a will after its execution. A codicil must be executed with the same formalities as the will itself.

cognitive impairment a limitation of one's ability to understand or to perceive.

co-insurance the percentage of a medical charge that a Medicare patient is required to pay.

community spouse resource allowance (CSRA) the total amount of a couple's assets the noninstitutionalized spouse is entitled to retain when one spouse applies for Medicaid benefits to finance nursing home care. The balance of the couple's assets is expected to be spent to support the spouse requiring institutional care.

conservator a person appointed for the purpose of managing the finances of a person who is incapable of managing for himself or herself. This leaves the individual free to make decisions about other aspects of life.

conservatorship the position and responsibilities of a conservator, appointed by a court.

constructive eviction when a tenant is forced by circumstances to move out, even if the landlord does not actually take steps to force the tenant to move. A fire that makes an apartment unlivable may create a constructive eviction, for example.

continuing care retirement community (CCRC) a residential facility that provides housing and other services, usually including some form of nursing home services, for a lifetime.

co-payment the portion of a medical or prescription charge that a patient is required to pay. Many HMOs, for example, have a flat charge per visit that patients pay when they see a plan doctor.

custodial care assistance with basic activities of daily living, such as bathing, dressing, and eating. This is in contrast to skilled nursing care, which addresses medical needs.

custody responsibility for the care and support of a minor child.

deductible the amount an insured person must pay yearly for medical services before his or her insurance begins to make payments.

defendant the person being sued in a civil lawsuit, as well as the person accused of a crime in a criminal case. In a civil lawsuit the person bringing the case is the plaintiff, so the opposing parties are plaintiff and defendant.

defined benefit retirement plan a retirement plan that provides pension benefits based on a formula considering such variables as an employee's years of service for the employer and his or her salary at the time of retirement.

defined contribution retirement plan a retirement plan that provides a fixed amount of funding from the employer for an employee's retirement. The contribution is usually a percentage of the employee's salary or some dollar amount that matches employee contributions, but once the employer contribution is made the employer has no further responsibility for the amount of pension received by the employee.

equity the difference between the value of a house and the mortgage against it.

exclusions conditions not covered by insurance by the terms of an insurance policy. For example, health insurance policies often exclude conditions that exist at the time of origination of the policy.

executor the person appointed by a will to administer the estate, including gathering all assets, paying debts, and distributing the assets in accordance with the terms of the will. For someone who dies without a will, the person who plays this role is an administrator.

fair hearing a hearing to determine one's rights regarding receipt of government benefits, including Medicare and Medicaid.

grievance a complaint.

guaranteed renewable with regard to insurance, a provision granting one the right to maintain a policy as long as the premiums are paid on time.

guardian a person appointed by a court to provide care for a person found to be incompetent to care for himself or herself.

guardianship the position and responsibilities of a guardian, who is appointed by a court to care for an incompetent person.

health care proxy the person appointed in an advance directive to make medical decisions for a person if there comes a time when the person cannot make those decisions for himself or herself.

heir a person who receives property under a will.

home equity the difference between the value of a home and the outstanding debts secured by the property.

home health services medical and nursing services provided in one's home.

homemaker services nonmedical services provided to help a person remain in his or her home and to avoid institutionalization.

hospice a program or facility providing supportive care for patients who are terminally ill and their families.

incapacitated unable to act for oneself.

intestate without a will. A person who dies without a will is said to have died intestate. When this happens New Jersey's law of intestate succession determines who receives his or her property, without regard to the individual's desires.

joint tenancy the condition of holding property in common with another person with a "right of survivorship," meaning that if one party dies, the property becomes the sole property of the other party.

lien (on property) a claim against property for the payment of a debt.

life care community a facility that provides housing and services for a person's lifetime. The specific services to be provided are defined by the terms of the contract with the facility.

living benefit rider a provision in a life insurance contract providing for benefits before death when the insured meets certain criteria.

long-term care the services provided at home or in a nursing home or other facility for a person who requires nursing or personal services for an extended period.

look-back period the period of time prior to an application for Medicaid that will be considered in determining what assets should be counted. If assets were transferred, the value of the assets may still be considered available to pay for care, even if they no longer belong to the applicant.

mediation a conflict resolution process that uses a neutral facilitator to attempt to bring all parties to an agreement to end the dispute.

medically needy having income above the level that would make one eligible for Medicaid, but medical costs that are so high that they have, in effect, reduced one's income below the eligibility level.

Medigap insurance a supplemental insurance policy that provides coverage for medical costs not paid for by Medicare, such as co-payments and deductibles.

overpayment a government benefits payment over and above that to which one is legally entitled.

peer review organization (PRO) a body that reviews the necessity of hospital care for Medicare recipients.

pension a fixed amount paid regularly by a former employer or the government after one retires.

plaintiff the party who initiates a civil lawsuit. The party making the initial complaint is the plaintiff, and the person being sued is the defendant.

power of attorney a document appointing one person to act for another. The person appointed is referred to as the other person's attorney in fact. Powers of attorney can be limited or broad. The extent of power of the attorney in fact is determined by the language of the document.

preexisting condition a medical condition that exists at the time one enters into an insurance contract. It is usually excluded from health insurance coverage, at least for a specific period of time.

premiums payments for insurance coverage.

public entitlement a government program that provides money or services to those who meet the established criteria.

qualified Medicare beneficiary (QMB) an individual or couple whose income falls below the federal poverty guidelines and whose assets fall below $4,000 for an individual or $6,000 for a couple, for whom the state will pay Medicare premiums, deductibles, and co-payments.

respite care services that allow a caregiver to take a break from caring for a relative or friend with a disability.

restraints chemical or physical devices used to limit the mobility and freedom of an institutionalized person.

reverse mortgage a loan that pays a home owner for the equity in the home, to be repaid at a later date, usually when the home owner dies or moves out of the house and it is sold.

security interest an interest in property that is held in order to ensure payment of a debt. When a loan is secured by a mortgage on a house, the lender holds an interest in the home in order to ensure the subsequent payment of the loan.

skilled nursing care treatment administered by a registered nurse or other professional therapist under the direction of a doctor.

special-needs trust a trust intended to provide for the needs of a person with a disability, without interfering with eligibility for government benefits.

specified low-income Medicare beneficiary (SLMB) an individual or couple whose income falls between 100 and 110 percent of the federal poverty guidelines and whose assets fall below $4,000 for an individual or $6,000 for a couple, for whom the state will pay the Medicare Part B premium.

testator a person who dies leaving a will.

vesting the right to a future pension, based on the terms of the program.

viatical settlement sale of a life insurance policy to receive benefits before the end of one's life.

visitation the right to visit a minor child on a court-ordered schedule.

waiver relinquishment of a right so that, if an overpayment is made, you may be able to persuade the government to give up its right to repayment.

weatherization services provided to maintain a house so that residents are protected. These may include roof repairs, window replacement, or other services.

Index

AARP. *See* American Association of Retired Persons

abuse of the elderly, 109–114; in nursing homes or institutions, 113–114

activities of daily living, 15, 41

adjustable rate loans, 148

administrator of estate, 62, 64

Adult Protective Services, 110, 112–113

adult retirement communities, 165–166

advance directives, 86–94; conditions for invoking, 87; sample, 88–93

age discrimination, 117–120; Age Discrimination in Employment Act (ADEA), 117, 118; filing a complaint, 119; mandatory retirement, 118; pensions and, 118; waivers, 119; who is protected, 118

agent (attorney in fact): appointed by power of attorney, 77, 78; power given to, 78

Aging, County Offices on, 173–177

alimony, 107

Alzheimer's Disease, 7; adult day care and, 32

American Association of Retired Persons (AARP), 143, 151

Americans with Disabilities Act, 117, 121; Social Security Disability Insurance claims and, 122

Anti-Eviction Act, New Jersey, 4, 155–156

appeals: home health care denials, 52; Medicare, 4, 22–24; Medicaid, 26–27; Social Security Disability Insurance, 13

Assisted Living Facilities Association, 171

assisted living residences, 166

assisted suicide, 38–39

attorney in fact: appointed by power of attorney, 77, 78; power given to, 78

attorneys: certified elder law attorneys, 55; employment attorneys, 120; fees in consumer cases, 132; fees for divorce, 107; when needed, 3

benefits, public, 7–34; estate planning and, 65

Better Business Bureau, 136, 139, 142

bills, assistance with water and sewer, 153, 162

Board of Mortuary Science, New Jersey, 142

boarding homes, 168

bona fide occupational qualification (BFOQ), 118

Bureau of Rooming and Boarding House Standards, 168

burial instructions. *See* funeral

CCPED. *See* Community Care Program for the Elderly and Disabled

CHIME. *See* Counseling on Health Insurance for Medicare Enrollees

Civil Rights, New Jersey Division of, 119, 122

COBRA. *See* Consolidated Omnibus Reconciliation Act of 1985 health insurance

combined advance directive for health care. *See* advance directives

Community Affairs, New Jersey Department of, 166, 168; CCRC Section, 167

Community Care Program for the Elderly and Disabled (CCPED), 28

community spouse resource allowance, 56

competency, 67–68

condominium conversion, 162–164

congregate housing services, 170

conservatorship, 96

About the Author

Alice K. Dueker is an attorney and the director of clinical programs at the Rutgers University School of Law–Camden, where she supervises the Civil Practice Clinic's Elder Law Project.